MIKE SCALISE

THE BRAND NEW CATASTROPHE

A MEMOIR

THE BRAND NEW CATASTROPHE

A MEMOIR

MIKE SCALISE

SARABANDE BOOKS LOUISVILLE, KY

This is a work of nonfiction. It is also a work of memory. I've researched the story to the best of my ability, and I've rendered the events to the best of my recall. I've compressed some aspects of the book's chronology, and for the sake of anonymity I've changed the names and details of some friends and all my doctors. Except for one. You'll know which.

Library of Congress Cataloging-in-Publication Data

Names: Scalise, Mike, author.
Title: The brand new catastrophe / Mike Scalise.
Description: Louisville, Ky : Sarabande Books, 2017. | Includes
bibliographical references and index.
Identifiers: LCCN 2016014119 (print) | LCCN 2016028132 (ebook) | ISBN
9781941411339 (paperback) | ISBN 9781941411346
Subjects: LCSH: Scalise, Mike. | Authors, American--Biography. | Scalise,
Mike--Health. | Brain--Tumors--Patients--Biography. | Sick--Psychology. |
Diseases--Humor. | Medical care--Humor. | Mothers and sons--Biography. |
MESH: Acromegaly--Patients--Biography. | BISAC: BIOGRAPHY & AUTOBIOGRAPHY
/ Medical. | HUMOR / Topic / Marriage & Family. | HISTORY / Social History.
Classification: LCC PS3619.C2547 Z46 2017 (print) | LCC PS3619.C2547 (ebook)
| DDC 818/.603--dc23
LC record available at https://lccn.loc.gov/2016014119

Cover design by Oliver Munday.
Interior and exterior design by Kristen Radtke.

Manufactured in Canada.
This book is printed on acid-free paper.

Sarabande Books is a nonprofit literary organization.

  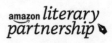

This project is supported in part by an award from the National Endowment for the Arts. The Kentucky Arts Council, the state arts agency, supports Sarabande Books with state tax dollars and federal funding from the National Endowment for the Arts.

For D., T., R., and L.

CONTENTS

PART ONE

PART TWO

PART THREE

PART FOUR

PART FIVE

PART SIX

Acknowledgments

You eke out your illness. You'll always be an amateur in your illness. Only you will love it.

—Anatole Broyard, *Intoxicated by My Illness*

PART ONE

PROLOGUE

A FRACTION OF A FRACTION
OF A FRACTION

Telling a good catastrophe anecdote means becoming a maestro of sympathy. People's reactions to these kinds of stories usually involve some defense mechanism: a tilting or nodding of the head, a crinkling of the brow, or the low-toned repetition of words and phrases like *wow, holy shit, oh no, sounds horrible*, or—and this is one to watch out for—*I'm just really glad you're okay.*

As the teller of the anecdote, the conductor of an experience, this is the wrong place to be. Any of those responses indicates that you've made yourself pitiable and taken your audience hostage. This is where they're likely to go on conversational autopilot, or retreat into head-nodding while they try to figure out what role to play in your *I had an awful thing happen to me* story. The trick to keeping them engaged is to focus on the oddities and ironies that would seem incredible and ridiculous in *any* context, not just that of your disaster.

For instance: The name of the doctor who discovered my brain tumor?

Sunshine.

He'd heard all the jokes. Of course he had. We met during hour six of an ER stay in Brooklyn, at a training hospital affiliated with an unremarkable university. I'd admitted myself for what I thought was a migraine—an undodgeable, wavelike cloud of pain that for the past nine hours had swished slowly to all ends of my brain. Sunshine was young and square-jawed, and introduced himself the way I imagined he greeted every new face, with a stiff handshake and a pursed tone—*I'm Dr. Sunshine*—that braced him like a boxer for every quip that swung back at him. Here was all I could think of:

"Get the fuck out of here."

He held the results of my CT scan, taken hours earlier.

"There's a mass on your brain," he said, then curled his forefinger and thumb into a circle that in any other context would mean A-OK. "We'll get a proper MRI first thing tomorrow," he told me. "We'll know more then."

"Is it the C-word?" I asked.

"Don't know yet."

"Am I going to die?"

"Don't know that yet either."

"I don't have insurance," I said.

"Let's not worry about that right now," he told me.

A hard surge tumbled along the banks of my skull.

"*Look*: just get it out," I told him. "Go grab a melon baller, and get it. The fuck. Out."

Sunshine called my parents in Pittsburgh and my girlfriend Loren, who was then on a trip to Los Angeles. He colluded with the hospital administrative staff to verify the bogus insurance arrangement my father quickly set up for me through my family's Pittsburgh-based heating and air-conditioning company. Then Sunshine admitted me upstairs, to a dimly lit floor with rounded walls. Patients' beds circled the admin desk like spokes, at least fifteen of them, separated only by thin, paperlike curtains.

There were pockets of quiet throughout the night, but eventually we seized on one another's discomfort and swung into a chorus of bickering that turned our nurses raw and curt and impatient. Any movement triggered ripples in my head pain, so I kept still and awake, rejecting all care that wasn't direct pain relief.

That included hygiene. In the morning, just before my MRI, a nurse appeared holding a small plastic stick loaded with toothpaste—no bristles—and pushed it at my face.

"Sir. You *must* brush your teeth," she said. "The smell from your mouth is very unpleasant."

Notice how the focus here is *not* on the vast pain that commandeered my head that night. Pain is a socially competitive thing, and too much emphasis on it can cue people to recall their own bouts with pain, or compare theirs to yours. Take, for instance, my mother, who walked, worry-shaken, into that

Brooklyn training hospital a veteran of her own burgeoning string of catastrophes, all of them heart-related. By age fifty she'd undergone two angioplasties and a bypass, and had partially lost sight in her left eye due to a blocked artery. She'd perfected the flat, dismissive tone in which she'd respond to anyone else's tale of woe, assuring them, in essence: *Take it easy, I've been through worse.*

Upon seeing me in that hospital bed, though, raw and clinched from the pain cavorting in my head, my mother thankfully set that tone aside, then looked for other ways to infuse the moment with her expertise. My parents arrived late morning, and I smelled the blend of cigarette smoke and drive-thru coffee that had fueled their night-long drive across Pennsylvania's highways. My father's hands were deep in the pockets of his cargo shorts. My mother gnawed on a fingernail. I dug into the sweat-ripe jeans on the chair next to my bed, then set the keys to my nearby apartment on the food tray between us. My parents returned an hour later, showered but not rested. My mother was holding a pillow from my bed. "These goddamn hospital pillows," she told me. "They're just glorified dish towels."

Dr. Sunshine had, by now, pushed me off to another doctor named Kalantari, a tall, slump-shouldered surgeon who confessed within minutes of meeting my parents that he'd actually done his med school internship in a hospital less than three miles from the house I grew up in, a lowly establishment in a depressed Pittsburgh suburb. That coincidence, that odd, local kinship, could have been why—as his team ran clumsy spinal taps and prepped me for a procedure scheduled for that very night—Dr. Kalantari appeared at my bedside, shifting, gripping a manila folder.

"Look," he told us. "This can be a simple procedure with the right resources. But let me put it this way: this hospital"— he tightened to a whisper—"is *not properly equipped* for what you need. I've contacted a neurosurgeon in Manhattan, the best in the country at this kind of thing. He's agreed to take you on. There's an ambulance on its way right now to take you to him. Please: don't say anything to anyone else here. Just get in that ambulance and *go*."

The simplest explanation goes like this. The mass on my brain and the headache it caused were a *pituitary apoplexy*, meaning that my head hurt that night because my brain was bleeding. It was late July of 2002, and at 2:00 A.M., when I'd woken in my Brooklyn apartment to take a piss, a hunk of tumor had ruptured in my head. The tumor had been clinging to the gland in my brain that controlled and dispensed hormones. Before the rupture the condition was called *acromegaly*, which meant that for a time I had too many hormones. After the rupture it was called *hypopituitarism*, which meant that at age twenty-four, just months out of college, I now had close to none.

For a long time, it was a predicament I understood only in terms of its rarity. Only 16 percent of diagnosed pituitary tumors secrete excess human growth hormone, or HGH, which causes acromegaly. And while it's not uncommon for pituitary tumors to experience apoplexy, the type of pituitary tumor I

had only ruptures 2 percent of the time. Plus: at 24 I was decades younger than the typical diagnosis age range of 49 to 53,
which meant that when I walked into the ER on that mouth-
warm July night, I became a fraction of a fraction of a fraction,
beckoning doctors, for years, to poke and prod and study me
like an abstract sculpture.

But avoid these kinds of details when you tell your catastrophe anecdote. Instead, go for crispness and entertainment.
Your goal is to sidestep any put-upon, sorry stares with a fine
payoff that eases the tension. So take a breath, leak out a smile,
then say something light and pithy, like:

That was almost fifteen years ago.

God, I miss that time.

See how that works?

CH. 1

THE DROWNING LIFEGUARD

A few months after my diagnosis I stood next to my mother in my parents' kitchen, our backs against the sink counter. It was 1:37 A.M. In one hand, she held a half-empty glass of iced Pinot Grigio, in the other an un-ashed cigarette. It was the first I'd seen her since my hospital stay, and my mother had some pointed feedback on the affair.

"You scared the *shit* out of me," she said.

"I know," I told her. "You just said that."

"You don't understand," she said.

"No. Mom. I do."

Her face was crumpled as if she were about to sneeze.

"No, you don't," she said. She waved her cigarette in front of herself like a conductor's baton. "You scared the *shit* out of me."

Some blurred version of my mother—petite, nervous, with

straw-blonde hair and a frame I've often heard her describe, accurately, as "bony"—exists in my childhood recollections as a resourceful, devoted, and generally happy parent. But that person was replaced in my adult years by someone new to me; someone who seemed content to be the defeated product of her snowballing illnesses. Every few months throughout my early twenties, doctors found her on the verge of some grand cardiopulmonary event, a fact she'd remind me of in these late night hours, head down and forlorn, repeating it until the wine and worry finally drove her eyes closed.

Which was why visits home became attempts at tactful avoidance. 12:30 A.M. was usually late enough to find her passed out next to my father on the living room couch: he snoring; she sitting upright, mouth wide; television flickering. But there were still nights like tonight, when there was no dodging the slow tack of her walk, the record skip of utterances that never found their way to her lips during the day.

"You just made *jokes* in that hospital," she said. She was almost crying now. Her teeth were clenched. "Had yourself a good old time," she said. "You scared the *shit* out of me."

"I know," I said. "I'm sorry."

"No. No. Michael. No," she said. She exhaled, closed her eyes, held her arm in the air as if hailing a cab, then swatted it down.

"You scared the *shit*—"

And so on.

What she may have been referring to: the secret ambulance from the Brooklyn training hospital delivered me to the brain trauma wing of a far more impressive facility in Upper Manhattan. My room had a view of the George Washington Bridge so pristine and breathtaking it felt like a vulgar intrusion of the chaos that had put me there to see it. Within hours I met Dr. Brian Elmer, a tall, bespectacled brain surgeon, and his band of underlings, who spread themselves in a silent crescent at the foot of my bed. As my neurosurgeon sketched out details—they'd slice an entryway in my upper gums, go through the nose cavity, then sneak in behind my eyeballs and yank out the tumor— my parents stood along the wall: my father heavy-lidded, my mother by his side, itchy-seeming, picking at her teeth with the folded cellophane from her soft pack of Marlboro Lights.

"The removal of the mass will leave a space inside your head," Elmer said. "Right behind the eyeballs. Of course we'll have to fill that."

The underlings nodded, scribbled notes. They were all assured and male, no more than a few years older than I was, which might have been why they later called me "man," "buddy," or "dude" while administering tests, or loosened their protocol when discussing the likelihood of post-op complications ("*Totally* minuscule," they said). The rupture had swollen my brain, so they'd given me Decadron, a pill that warded off the ache and swelling with stunning efficiency. I was clear now, alert.

"What," I asked Elmer, "will you fill the space in my head with?"

"Fat deposits," he said. "We'll either take them from the side of your leg or the back of your thigh."

"*Back of my thigh*," I said. "You mean my ass?"

"Well," he said. "The back of your thigh."

"So you mean my ass," I said.

"Sure, okay," he said. "But we'll likely take the fat from the side of your leg."

"No," I said, to him and then to everyone. "Take it from my ass. *I want my ass in my head.*"

One of the underlings let out a mini-snort. My father gasped *shit-head!* like he'd arrived at the answer of a long-unsolved riddle. As I spat out something half-baked about wanting "a bona-fide excuse for all future mistakes," my mother exhaled and chomped down on a fingernail.

"Shit for brains," I told Dr. Elmer. "Say you can make that happen."

I drove my orderlies weary with a line I'd beat to death in the coming years.

"We're going to take some quick blood samples," they'd say.

"Make it quick," I'd tell them. "My head's about to explode."

I entered into an over/under game with my pleasant, Dominican nurse, Avis, regarding how many bad rental car jokes she'd heard from patients during her rounds.

"Avis!" I'd say. "So what are we at now? Three?"

"Depends," she'd say. "Does this count as one?"

The morning after I arrived, three days into the affair, Avis wheeled me to the Visual Field Test station located, almost like a closet, in the back room of the hospital's nursery. I'd taken my first VFT while still in Brooklyn, still under the unbearable throttle of my apoplexy. The pulse of the swollen tumor had pushed against the backs of my eyeballs, cloaking my periphery in waves of dense, cloudlike illuminations. I saw only what was directly in front of me. Now, post-Decadron, I pressed my face against that set of closed binoculars with a painless clarity and a renewed vigor. Spots of light appeared on a blackened backdrop for me to pinpoint: to the left, lower left, upper right, etc., and I pounced on them like whack-a-moles. The technician—a soft-spoken woman named Jean who appeared to be in her late forties—ambled into a conversation:

"You still in college?"

"Just got out in January. *Upper left.*"

"Oh, well that's nice."

"My parents would certainly agree," I said. "I was on what they like to call the five-point-five-year plan. Upper right. *Upper right.*"

We moved on to small talk about hopes and career intentions that I'd come to find grating and learned to avoid after six months of unemployment in New York. But with my head clear, every familiar thing felt like a reward. Jean said she had a daughter a few years younger than me who was thinking about being an English major, like I'd been. I told her I hadn't had a job in six months—*left. Lower right*—and that she should double major in something useful and employable (how about neurosurgery?)—*right. Lower left*—then I reeled off canned one-liners about head explosions and shit for brains—*left. Upper left.*

My operation was the next morning, so that afternoon my mother, father, and I sat subdued in my hospital room, quietly watching a repeat marathon of *The Thomas Crown Affair* on the tiny television that hung over my bed like a crane arm. My mother was talking about how superior the original 1968 version was—how it was the first movie she and my father had seen together when they began dating in high school, how they loved it so much they went back the next week—when Jean the VFT tech arrived at my room. She placed a plastic bag on the swivel tray next to that day's empty dinner plate. Inside the bag was a box of green and blue thatched stationary and three matching steel pens.

"So you can do your writing," Jean said.

Then she leaned in for a light, careful hug.

My mother spent the rest of the evening lapsing into sobs while playing Trivial Pursuit to pass time. She chain-smoked on the curb of the hospital valet ("forty-five dollars *a day* it cost us to park there," she'd remind me during a future late night ramble). According to later reports from my father, she made demanding, unsuccessful calls to her sister in Jersey—"I *need* you here"—then spent the remaining nights of my hospital stay awake well into the morning hours, flooding my overheated railroad apartment with hovering layers of cigarette smoke, perhaps recalling her own memories of hospitals, and thinking, with good reason:

Is he actually enjoying this?

My tumor's rupture wasn't the first time I scared the shit out of my mother. That happened seven years before when, during the peak of my tenure as Head Lifeguard for the local public swimming pool and captain of my high school varsity swim team, my mother received a call from school officials informing her that I had drowned.

It occurred during "swim class," a phys ed requirement for juniors, taught by my coach, Jane McCarty—a crass, leather-tan woman who wore only jean shorts, regardless of the season, and kept a box of Marlboro reds rolled in the sleeve of her T-shirt. (Year: 1995.) She'd set up a series of weekly skill tests for our class to complete in order to pass: The "head-first dive." The "one-length freestyle sprint." "Water polo." The one that claimed me was the "underwater swim," which she evaluated based on how long one could stay submerged while swimming:

Half the pool (12.5 yards) = C
3/4 of a length (18.75 yards) = B
One full length (25 yards) = A

She announced it on a Monday, four days before the test, as we filed out of the thick, muggy pool. But before I was out of earshot she clapped her hands and yelled out: "MICHAEL. TWO AND A HALF LENGTHS FOR YOU, OR YOU DON'T PASS THIS CLASS. YOU HEAR ME?"

I wasn't the fastest swimmer on the varsity team, not even close, but I had notoriously powerful lungs. At the end of practices Coach McCarty made us sit for as long as possible with five-pound diving bricks at the bottom of the shallow end of the pool. The last one up would receive some lighter form of torture the following day. It was always me. While the rest of my teammates tried hard to break the thirty-seconds mark, I ditched the diving brick, then crawled around to each of them and broke their cool: wedgies, thumb jabs, underwater moons. "Michael," McCarty would say above water, "you've got to quit fuckin' around, hon."

A year before, when I was a sophomore, McCarty pulled me from my gym class to her junior swimming class in order to teach a handful of nervous, eligibility-seeking football players how to do elementary backstroke. In return she let me dominate the skills tests. "Your goal today," she'd say to everyone, "is to *not* let Michael kick your ass again." I entered the "underwater swim" that year expecting only to be obnoxious—I knew from practice that I could make one length easy—but when I got to the *two*-length point, the amount of gas I had left surprised me. So I pushed off the wall again, and came to the surface at two and a half lengths (62.5 yards), my lungs tight like fists.

I knew immediately I'd never do it again.

Over the next twelve months I entered into a strong friendship with Jeff Stibner—a loud, magnetic, and inappropriate fellow backstroker—that revolved around weekends of *NHL Hockey* on Sega Genesis, Ned's Atomic Dustbin CDs on repeat, scavenged alcohol, and makeshift bongs built from tinfoil and empty Coke bottles. Coach McCarty caught me twice at swim meets sneaking smokes (stolen from my mother) outside the pool area during the distance events, and had pulled me into her office along with Jeff and the rest of my medley relay team after we showed up to Saturday morning practice perfumed in (my mother's) beer. I went from a favored pupil to someone McCarty felt betrayed by and suspicious of, and even though the season was over, she seemed intent to retaliate by hijacking my grade in the only class in which I was a ringer. Her refrain was *two and a half or you don't pass*, and in the days leading up to the "underwater swim," she repeated it with her sharp, raspy twang every time I walked by. That Thursday I stopped by her office with Jeff (also in my swimming class, also a subject of suspicion) and a few other team members to drop off sponsor sheets for an upcoming fundraiser, and midconversation she said:

"Did you all hear? Michael's doing his fancy two-and-a-half-length underwater trick tomorrow. That or he gets a big, fat F."

Then she locked eyes with me and smiled.

"I mean it, hon. See you tomorrow."

The last thing I thought as my legs shoved off the wall after the second length, ribcage screaming, was: *My lungs: not what they were a year ago.*

When she learned of her first heart procedure in 1999—an angio-plasty in which a surgeon inflated a small balloon in one of her clogged arteries, then inserted a ringlike stent to keep the passage from closing—my mother called a family meeting on the back porch of our house where she, my father, my younger brother, and I sat in a semicircle of lounge chairs.

She began her speech at near collapse: "Nothing to panic over . . . completely routine procedure . . . in and out in a day or two . . . ninety-nine percent blockage," and she was in tears by its end. She said that "it was okay to be scared," but we were hardly shocked by the news. Her lineage had been telegraphed for years. My grandfather, my mother's father, had died of a heart attack while working on a railroad before I was born, and in recent years her older sister in New Jersey had been accruing her own collection of heart ailments, operations, and procedures. The only person who seemed blindsided by the diagnosis was my mother, and it was a blow that she struggled during those years to get up from.

It was late May—three years before my apoplexy—and I'd moved back in with my parents for the summer to save money while I worked a low-paying internship. I watched as my mother, both in practice and in spirit, resigned herself to the ugliest scenarios her doctors had drawn out for her. The grim, impenetrable tones of her late night sermons drove both my father and me weary with impatience. She smoked and drank now with a morbid theatricality.

We both attempted to talk to her during sober hours. We implored her to quit smoking and drink less, to take up an exercise regimen. We told her we were worried, that her life depended on a very manageable set of changes. But each time she lashed out in such loud, convincing fits of despair—hands in the air and actual, deadly serious wailing at the top of her lungs—that my father and I became ruled by the likelihood that she might do something terrible to herself in response to our confrontations. By August we entered into a wordless, laissez-faire attitude toward her behavior that bordered on resentment.

Fine. Kill yourself, we seemed to say.

Watch me, she seemed to say back.

Two deaths cast a shadow over the year I nearly drowned. One was that of my grandmother—my mother's mother—who had a stroke, quickly deteriorated, found herself in an assisted-living facility, then died. The other was Chrissy Davis, who sat two desks behind me in Advanced Algebra and found herself in a car accident, then a coma, then also died.

I barely knew Chrissy. She seemed like a promising sophomore regarded mostly for her meekness and smarts, and in a matter of weeks the events surrounding her death had gone from seeming shocking to seeming inevitable. Chrissy wasn't a popular student, but her death provoked a mournful, nebulous air that floated through my high school hallways and softened everyone's edges: assemblies were held. A row of small trees was dedicated to her memory and planted on the thin strip of grass in front of the school administrators' parking lot.

By the time I nearly drowned that April, much of the student body had been primed for months with the concepts of grief and demise, which meant that when Jeff Stibner showed up at the hospital the afternoon of my near drowning with a grin and said, "So: I've been telling everyone you're dead," the news took on a quicker and more serious momentum than either of us anticipated. For each of the two days that I rested at home, my mother fielded a number of calls from girls I'd "gone with" in middle school, teachers, and complete strangers calling to offer their condolences. "He's eating dinner right now," she told the last few. "I'll let him know."

From home I basked in the deception, but I was unsure how to respond to the raw purity of the well-wishes that greeted me when I arrived back at school. I was a student of midlevel popularity, a B-list guy at best, but people now stopped their conversations for double takes or to slap my hand. Girls gave me hugs. Teachers I never took classes with told me how glad they were that I was "still with us." By sixth period I was asked about the incident so often that my physics teacher, Mr. Nemchek, let me commandeer his lesson on torque and rotation to tell my story to the class in hopes that it would ripple out and set the record straight.

It went like this. After pushing off the wall following my second length, I passed out underwater somewhere around the sixty-yard mark, drifted briefly to the surface, then sunk immediately to the bottom. This was according to Jeff Stibner, whom Jane McCarty ordered to "go in there and tell Michael to stop fuckin' around" after about thirty seconds of what she must have thought was a superhuman game of possum. Jeff—whose face I'd often taunted with my bare ass during diving-brick drills—thought I was joking too, and brought me to the surface like a baby, he said, cradling me in his arms and cooing as the rest of the class watched on.

"But then," Jeff told me later, "I saw that your lips were blue," at which point the whole situation probably would have benefited from the help of a trained lifeguard. No one had ever seen Jane McCarty in the water—fueling speculation that the varsity swim coach did not, in fact, know how to swim—which meant that perhaps the only person there qualified to handle the situation was actually me.

Standard Red Cross lifesaving protocol for a situation like this would have been to (1) hook the victim from behind, under the armpits, (2) drag him to the side of the pool, (3) place his hands on deck, (4) climb out, then lift him by the arms, cushioning the head with your foot as you (5) lay the victim face-first on the surface before carefully pulling his legs up out of the water. But Jeff Stibner called in P. J. Tedesco, a stalky classmate with a curious devotion to Dan Marino, and together the two, almost like a soccer throw-in, lifted me up above their heads and tossed my unconscious body over the high lip of the pool's edge and onto the deck.

I awoke to the crisp smell of Marlboros over chlorine. Jane McCarty hovered over my face.

"MICHAEL. HOW MANY FINGERS DO I HAVE UP, HON. HOW MANY FINGERS."

She held up four. So I said, "Four."

"OKAY WHAT DAY IS IT. TELL ME WHAT DAY IT IS."

It was Friday. So I said, "Friday."

"LAY HERE. DON'T MOVE."

I have a test in Physics, I thought. *Can't be late for that.*

"I have to go to Physics," I said, and leaned forward to sit up.

"UNH-UH, HON. CAN'T DO THAT."

"OK," I said, "then I'm going back to sleep."

"OH NO NO NO NO HEY NO NO NO NO—"

It was raining, and the ambulance pulled up onto the muddy grass outside of the pool, near the one-way doors we routinely threw rookies out of during Christmas break workouts. After being submerged underwater for something like two minutes—new personal record—I was cloaked by an EMT in a silver hypothermia blanket that I didn't feel for two hours, transferred onto a stretcher, then into the back of the ambulance. As the driver turned the engine over, the EMT prepared an IV (which I reacted to with a fear that I can only characterize now as *very cute*). "I have fifty dollars somewhere," I said to him, "and I will find it and give it to you if you don't give me that IV."

I felt the hum of the tires below me, but we weren't moving. The ambulance wheels had sunken so deeply into the muddy grass that the coach summoned a number of my classmates and the school security guard, who radioed Mr. Mitchell, my sociology teacher, and Bob Meredith, the principal, to swarm the scene and help a pack of seventeen-year-old boys in swimsuits rock an ambulance forward to the hospital. Inside, the EMT gripped my arm by the wrist, held the IV needle over a vein on the back of my hand—"*Seriously*," I pleaded, "fifty bucks"—and waited for the cab to steady, which took what felt like twenty minutes. According to Jeff Stibner, all nine people who pushed the ambulance out were blanketed in chunks of mud by the time the siren cleared the way to the hospital.

Jane McCarty showed up there no more than an hour later, and didn't leave until my parents wheeled me out that evening.

The story was a hit. My physics class gave it a bold ovation. Jen Wheeler, a senior, came up to me after the bell rang, mussed my hair, and said, "Thanks for that, Scalise."

It was like that for days. *Tell it again,* everyone asked, so I did. In some versions Jeff and P. J. took several tries to get me over the lip of the pool's edge, banging my head like a battering ram off of the porcelain deck tiles, but it remained a tale of survival in spite of the less-than-stellar choices made by nearly every person connected to it. Jane McCarty, ruled by guilt, called me every evening for drawn-out conversations so unbearably sincere that I eventually refused to pick up. Mr. Mitchell, one of the teachers who shoved off my ambulance, typed me a one-page, single-spaced letter applauding the "grace in which you handled yourself following the incident." But there were detractors, too. Ms. Ingram, another gym teacher—my high school had a quorum of them—allegedly took the opportunity to explain to her class what an "idiot" I was, and how I "deserved to drown."

Maybe they were all right, maybe nobody was. I didn't care. The reactions had little to do with me. Chrissy Davis's death had exposed a mob of nervous, desperate teens to the cold outcome of a tragic arc. Four months later, here was one that actually worked out well. I was just a conduit for an accident narrative, and filled a need for redemption that many in my high school longed to experience. What surprised me was how *electric* it felt to be that conduit. Any lingering fear, embarrassment, regret, or hesitation I had couldn't find room amidst the lovely, kinetic clamor surrounding my accident, so I took the opportunity to wrap myself in a myth as I constructed it. The Drowning Lifeguard. I polished it for weeks; perfected the beats and ironies, tweaked the lines, heightened the moments. In one telling, the EMT jabbed at my skin with the IV needle, lost his balance, then fell on his ass in the back of the cab (partially true). In another, I was placed in a hospital bed next to someone who, in a fit of rage, defecated on the floor (also true, sort of). As I told the story to friends at basement drinking parties, to girls on dates, to my parents' friends, to my relatives, I reveled in my budding aptitude for the passive art of survival. It was a neat trick: the *story* became the star of the show, while the person at its core—the one with tiny puddles of water in his once pristine-lungs, the twelve-year competitive swimmer who'd go swimming again only a handful of times over the next decade—disappeared.

I sometimes wonder: *What were my mother and I before our disasters?* There's a flash of me, very young, sitting at the kitchen table next to her, head on my crossed forearms, silent as she read and smoked (Salems then), me trying to dodge the cobweb of cigarette smoke that crept from the ashtray toward my face, still trying to stay close to her. I remember her forcing me to read *To Kill a Mockingbird* the summer before fourth grade, and me lying that August and saying I did. I recall weeks of anticipation as she assembled, from scratch, a near-replica Spider-Man Halloween costume when I was nine: a form-fitted mask with full-vision eyeholes. She assembled and stitched it on a Styrofoam wig display, made expansions and alterations based on my own head shape. Every webbed line down the arms and chest was identical to the illustrations in my comics—the outfit so durable, to scale, and impressively detailed that I kept it for years after I was far too big to wear it, next to the rest of my clothes, like it might one day come of use. My mother tore through books, thick ones, two to three a week (favorites: *Cold Sassy Tree*, *Lonesome Dove*). She got certified as a swimming referee, then judged the starts and turns or shot the starter pistol at nearly every swim meet I can remember participating in. She made an incredible, buttery shrimp bisque, had a pronounced weakness for chocolate-covered caramel turtles, was unbeatable at Scrabble, and loved, when someone asked her "What's up?" to reply, snottily, with "The sky. A preposition."

Beyond that, I remember competition. Slap-boxing matches in the living room during my preteen years to "toughen me up." "Hit me back!" she'd bark as I stood, guard barely raised, her bony hands snapping harder and faster across my cheek, chin, eye, me paralyzed with confusion, letting it happen, even as I grew taller than her. (How hard, exactly, should one slap one's own mother?) She was a quick study, loud and incredulous when my father and I couldn't understand simple logic or mechanics. She often talked about how her late father— who seemed from stories like a childish, easily threatened man—believed women had no place in college and forbade his daughters to go. When I was tested a high IQ in my early years and then struggled with math and science nearing high school, my mother responded by holding evidence of her own academic promise over my head.

"I *bet* you won't do better than I did," I heard. "Top of my class, and I wasn't even *in* the smart classes like you," she said. "I'll dig up the grades. You won't do better. I bet you won't."

I hated it, all of it. By high school I'd become sullen and melancholy, my grades middling, my prospects even more so. Anything to not engage, to leave my mother's challenges unanswered.

But when it came to my drowning junior year, I was surprised at how stingy and protective I became over the incident, how eager I was to finally stand some ground with the woman. In the weeks after I was fished from the pool, my mother and I entered into a strange and fierce battle of constitutions about who had copyright to the narrative of my rescue. The more I told the tale of The Drowning Lifeguard, the more she attempted to trump it. I'd never seen my mother attend a religious event that wasn't a wedding or a funeral, but during those weeks she became convinced of my grandmother's heavenly, guardian hand.

"Your *grandmother* was the one who pulled you out of that pool, you know," my mother said.

"Pretty sure it was Jeff Stibner, Mom."

Just a year earlier, my mother had been a key decision-maker in the move of my grandmother from the small home she had lived in for four decades to an assisted-living compound in the gravelly back lot of a run-down strip mall a mile away. When she died a few months after, it struck my mother as an act of consequence. She assumed all responsibility, even though the outcome was imminent and achingly telegraphed for two years. Then in her late sixties, my grandmother had done next to nothing to improve her health following her stroke. She smoked *more* Salems, drank *more* peach schnapps. Sitting on a couch next to her became a bizarre exercise in human puddling: Once a spry, southern belle–type, she began upright, but within minutes her body slackened and her waist dripped over the edge of the cushion, legs loose and bent, as if she was trying to sneak, undetected, into her own grave.

No matter. My mother absorbed the fault and became convinced that my grandmother might have somehow regenerated her old form, had she remained in the accustomed environment. At seventeen I became the reluctant audience to a series of late night speeches about fate and blame that either started or ended with the phrase "I killed your grandmother." Nothing my father or I said convinced my mother otherwise.

"*Fine,*" I finally told her one night, both of us standing in the kitchen. She was crying. "You did. You killed her. All you, Mom. Totally your fault."

"Well!" she said. "Okay then!" and started to laugh, so I built the case against her that she seemed to want constructed, and laid it out with as much conviction as I could fake: it was *her* neglect, *her* decision-making, and so on. My mother closed her eyes, still laughing, then gave me a tight hug, harder than I'd ever had from her. I put my arm around her and patted her head lightly, which seemed like the right thing to do.

"Thank you," she said, her thin arms snug around my waist like a belt. Then she thanked me again, and again, and again.

But after my drowning, my grandmother's rescue powers became the constant, maddening subject of my mother's late night rhetoric. I'd developed a pronounced sense of myself as a nonreligious person, and took the insistence as an affront to my core belief system.

"The universe has something far greater in store for me," I told her one night, with a straight face and everything. For both of us, the event of my drowning took on a form that had little to do with me. For my mother, it became an opportunity to be haunted, and she seemed grateful for it.

Skip ahead seven years and three heart procedures, swap the setting from a kitchen to an Upper Manhattan hospital room, and still: the same players, two hams beneath the spotlight of personal disaster. During my first night in the brain trauma ward, my mother came unwound ("You scared the *shit* out of me"). And because she'd trained me to slap her back, and because it was the only swing I ever threw that landed, I countered with my bad puns, shit jokes, and fresh stationery, sitting upright in my bed with my legs crossed under me, flirting with the female nurses, having something that looked like fun.

But I had only one blueprint—my drowning—and I quickly learned that little of this new catastrophe matched up with the first one. After I drowned I was able to paint myself the victim of my own hubris or idiocy (pick one, maybe both?), but here I didn't seem to have that advantage, and I struggled in the early hours at the brain trauma ward to locate a proper tenor. (If an almost-drowning is a "near miss," what then is a ruptured brain tumor that doesn't kill you?)

After Jean the VFT tech left my hospital room, hormone doctors invaded. They were led by Dr. Parsens, a waif with tightly pulled hair and blank eyes. Like my neurosurgeon, she brought an entourage of subspecialists. Hers were uniformly female, uniformly humanoid. They stood at my bedside with flat expressions, clipboards to their chests or hands clasped in front of them.

Parsens held up a sheet of paper on which she'd drawn a brain inside a head. On it was a scribbled dot labeled PITUITARY. She explained that the gland sits at the base of the brain, behind the eyes, the king gland of the endocrine factory. The pituitary was, she said, the silent dictator of our lifeblood, our body's smallest, most prescient multitasker: at once an interpreter and a messenger. Along with the hypothalamus, it senses our potential for human experience, then triggers the glands in its employ to *get ready*, to prime our bloodstream with hormones that permit us to feel and maneuver our way through things like love, hunger, sex, and sleep fully and naturally with zero thought as to why. Without the pituitary's commands, the rest of our endocrine system stalls, Parsens said, just a line of ready soldiers waiting for orders.

Next to PITUITARY on the diagram, Parsens wrote the words ANDROGENS and HUMAN GROWTH HORMONE. The second one she circled twice.

"The tumor is currently overproducing growth hormone and has been for some time," she said. She went on to say that in a typical tumorectomy, GH levels—along with the rest of one's hormonal portfolio—return to normal almost immediately. "But we don't know for how long excess GH has been secreting, and we won't be able to tell the kind of damage the rupture has done to the pituitary," Parsens said. "Not until after."

She detailed my future in the brain trauma wing as one of near-constant tests and gaugings. Every word sounded like some jagged other-tongue, a montage of alien jargon that built to a dull momentum. *Secretions. IGF-1 counts. Diabetes insipidus.* Parsens wrote the words FOLLICLE STIMULATING HORMONES on her diagram and began talking about their functions, which were, I understand now, largely female and reproductive. But all I heard then were the words "follicle" and "stimulation," which made me think quickly of my plain, smooth face, one that looked far younger than my twenty-four years.

"Brass tacks," I said. "Does this mean I'll finally be able to grow a suitable beard? I've never been able to," I told her. "Figured it was hormonal. Do we have that technology? Can we make that a reality?"

"That," Parsens said, "is not how it works."

CH. 2

MORE RECENT UNFINISHED BUSINESS

*E*ach catastrophe gives birth to its own universe of loved ones, friends and acquaintances, all pulled into a troubled orbit around the busted person at its core. In those first hospital days there were rare calls from relatives that revealed trite, political motives ("I would have called earlier had your mother *told* me, you know . . ."), but most were genuine, helpful, and laced with bad Schwarzenegger impressions ("It's *NAHT* a too-mah"). There were get-well cards, silly gifts. Longtime family business clients sent me nonperishables in baskets. While my mother looked for new ways to whip herself into a froth of agita, seeming close to tears for even basic, low-stakes conversations like that night's hospital meal, my younger brother—then on a trip to Maryland with friends he'd recently graduated high school with—inherited, begrudgingly, the part of Absentee Sibling, due in no small part to my insistence. *No, please, stay put. Do not come to New York. Enjoy yourself, I'm fine.* Like he had for my mother's procedures, my father reassumed the role of Ambassador of Information, dispatching details to concerned parties with as much recall as his aptitude allowed.

"No, not an aneurysm," I'd hear him say over the phone, ruffling through notes. "It was a rupture on the—wait, what does that say?—*shit*, can't read my own handwriting."

He gave many of those updates to Loren, who spent every moment after Dr. Sunshine's phone call on standby lists in West Coast airline terminals, jockeying for a seat on the soonest flight to LaGuardia. She'd been in Los Angeles for four days visiting friends, and it was the first time in our six months living together that I'd been alone in New York City. I was ill-prepared on all fronts. My bank balance was anemic. I roamed the pockets of Brooklyn with no destination, walked alongside the Gowanus Canal only to turn on a dime when I found myself abruptly in unwelcome neighborhoods. I took trips to small, homey bookstores and talked fiction with the clerks, too ashamed or exhausted to ask if they had an opening. I trolled the vast, wall-spanning magazine racks at bookstore chains and stared longingly at rows of monthlies ranging from *Esquire* to *Creative Knitting*, thinking, *One of these places must need a copy-editor or a fact-checker or a freelance something.*

But they didn't. Nobody did. My days to that point had been a regimen of fruitless line-casting spelled only by bad daytime television. Once Loren left for LA, I applied to no jobs for the first time in half a year. The sink filled with food-clotted dishes.

I drank beer, left the empties throughout the apartment, and did nothing when our AC unit broke under the cruel weight of that July heat, leaking exhaust onto a pile of dirty clothes I'd wrangled together on the floor of our bedroom, filling the air of the place with an acrid, mold-Freon twinge. The New York experiment, I knew now, was a failure. I wondered at what point Loren might come to the same conclusion about me.

Loren and I had been together for as long as I'd been in college, the sweeping majority of which we spent at universities hours apart from one another. We'd coupled up during the waning months of high school, following a conspicuous friendship that elevated on a drunk New Year's Eve, then quickly gave way to skipped school days spent tangled up in her bed. Loren was driven and firm-minded and pissed and over high school. She and her best friend kept a joint notebook they labeled THE BOOK OF BITTERNESS in which they cataloged detestable teen ephemera: deflating comments from boys, slights from teachers and coaches. Loren wanted out of high school, and so did I, and we liked that about each other in more ways than we understood, then, what to do with. But while I coped by disengaging, she trained herself to project a kind of early-onset adulthood; this irresistible aura of militant competence that seemed to say *I have no use for any of this.* Before me she'd dated college guys, or older boys in prep schools far from ours. She carried herself with such a raw command through our high school's hallways that more than once underclassmen mistook her for a teacher. At our prom, which she was loath to attend, she wore a navy jumpsuit with palazzo pants. Teachers and other parents liked to tell her how "together" she seemed, and Loren found snide, tremendous ways to give them a middle finger, too.

"And what will you study in college?" they'd ask.

"I hear I talk to people quite well," she'd say.

"So communications then?"

"No, conversations," she'd say, straight-faced. "I'm going to hire myself out for parties as a freelance conversationalist."

Me: I was stick thin and unsure, with a shark-fin nose and middling prospects—I wanted, I told people then, to be a writer, though I could count on one hand the amount of books I'd read. ("I don't want anyone else's work to influence my own," was the reasoning, and I actually said that to people). Yet when I pressed Loren about why she felt so strongly about me, she'd smile and say only, "You've got potential." Shortly before we graduated high school—both of us set to attend colleges a state apart, her for international business and French, me to study the language I already spoke—we sat eye to eye in the sagging middle of her waterbed, our legs entwined, foreheads close.

"I need you to know," she said, "that I'm in this for the long haul."

"Definitely," I said. "Me too." Then we entered into a five-year bout of what half-drunk people at our respective universities referred to derisively as a "long-distance relationship" (or, when they felt clever, an "LDR"). Our families had similar attitudes. We liked to keep a tally of the ways they hinted subtly, then not so subtly, that we should diversify our engagements. We didn't care. We saw it all as fuel for our union. "We do this better than everyone else," Loren would say when we visited each other for weekends, which we spent locked beneath bedcovers, sketching out our adult plans, all built on the same hubris and mild contrarianism we used to justify our LDR. *New York City, no marriage, no kids. Just us, just this.* It became our refrain, one we relied more heavily on as our college experiences fell further out of sync. Loren stayed on track, but I became a collegiate nomad (5.5 years = 2 state schools, 1 community college. Grade point average: unmentionable), and though Loren moved to Brooklyn a year and a half before I did, in the summer of 2000, to take a job at a Manhattan consulting firm, little changed in her vision of what we would or should be.

Yet by the time I got there on the first day of 2002, the backdrop of that vision had, of course, warped tremendously. She'd been placed on "forced sabbatical" from her job in the weeks following September 11th. She'd taken two part-time gigs, each within blocks of our apartment: one as a pastry maven at a tiny bakery, the other a cocktail waitress at a tavern called Angry Wade's. I found quickly that of the things New York needed to rebuild its strength, another middling English major was not one of them. Within weeks I exhausted my graduation money and help from relatives. My lone social act—the only one I could afford—was to barfly Loren's shifts at Wade's, where I sipped comped beers and listened to laid-off IT managers so stripped of themselves that they had to move back into their parents' Bed-Stuy basements; producer-level TV vets reduced to jobs as pages and interns—all of us lousy with the same dumb weight—until Loren peeled me away for the 4:00 A.M. walk home.

We fought more than we ever had. And the fights were boring. Everything we did was boring and cliché, and the fact that we were failing at it only magnified its banality. We fought about dishes and toilet seats and who held the remote—stock couple-isms that we'd spent the last five years mocking—but mostly we fought about what we weren't doing, what we weren't *able* to do. For the first time there was a wall between us and what we'd hoped for, one we couldn't topple, so we turned our frustration on the next closest thing: one another. Days before she left for Los Angeles, days before my tumor ruptured, we spent a summer afternoon sequestered in our bedroom, wringing ourselves dry. Loren was back-flat on the hardwood, teary and surrendered; me on the bed, head between my knees. I'd snapped at her for complaining, as she often did, that she couldn't get a management job in the nonprofit sector.

"Know what? I can't even get *a* job. You? You have *two*," I said.

She responded with silence, a non-response, not even a look into my eyes.

"Maybe I should just go to Boston," I told her.

My Republican cousin lived there. He had offered to get me something "entry level" in what he called "biotech."

"Do it," Loren said, then walked out of the room.

We didn't argue again in the days before she boarded her flight, but we didn't apologize to one another, either. By the time I woke at 1:00 A.M. to take the piss that would deliver me to Dr. Sunshine, by the time that pain fell like a molten, cracked egg down the inside of my skull, I'd already become convinced Loren would arrive home to find me couch-bound in our living room, then ask—as calmly and as assuredly as she'd once said, "You've got potential"—for me to pack my bags for anywhere else.

Where she actually found me was on a gurney in a recovery room, four days after my tumor's rupture, and two days into my stay in the Upper Manhattan hospital. It was early afternoon. I was just out of the operating room and far from awake, gauze jammed deep and wide into the wells of my nostrils, a handlebar mustache of thick, dry blood sketching my swollen face. She'd landed shortly before my surgery team wheeled me down for anesthesia, then cabbed to the brain trauma ward at once. When Avis and the nurses cleared me for visits, my father escorted her into the recovery room—a room that appears only in my mind now as awash in dull white—where Loren turned ghostly, buckled hard at the knees. My father, I discovered later, caught her limp body as she dropped, unconscious, toward the tile floor.

I saw Loren a few minutes later, my eyes now as open as my senses, which wasn't very much at all. The inside of my mouth was rubbered over with dryness, the pockets of my eyeballs glued down by the residue of anesthesia. Loren held a cup of tap water with one hand and gripped the steel bar of my gurney with the other, her soft face weary, blushless and brimming with unease.

I reached out for her, then asked, very gently, if she wanted to make out.

The hospital crew moved my tiny universe to a new room in a new section of the brain trauma ward, and if there was a glorious view from its windows I never saw it. Neurosurgery upsets the thin moat of spinal fluid that encases the brain, triggering your body to produce more of it, so I was ordered by my surgeon to lie still in a chaise-lounge position, the back of my head pinned to my pillow. For the excess spinal fluid, my surgeons installed a valve at the base of my back, like a tapped maple, and every twenty minutes Avis came to my room to release it. It felt incredible, every time, like letting loose a soul-deep sneeze.

But there was little Avis could do for the spinal fluid that flowed in tiny streams through the dam of my nostril gauze, catching on the rim of my top lip. (I loved touching my tongue to it, warm and salty like tears or seawater.) I was ordered to lie reclined until it all dried—estimate: four days—after which my surgery team would, hopefully, deem me fit for discharge. I had a roommate now, an old, sinewy man whose multiple brain tumors had stacked upon themselves and knocked him into a pendulum sway of dementia. His tiny universe consisted of his son and daughter, both seemingly in their early forties, with shorts and white legs and thick Queens accents. They attempted to feed their father ice cream sandwiches—which they tried to remind him were his favorite snacks—and each time he swatted them away like a colicky infant, demanding his children state their names. Avis called him "Grandpa." He'd twist and turn and writhe in his bed like a feeding alligator, stripping off his sheets and gown and tubes, until Avis came in to say, "Grandpa is naked again!" or: "Grandpa pulled out his catheter again!"

As a matter of distraction, my father assigned himself the task of locating a clear station on the tiny television by my bed. The only option was CNN, now midway through day-long coverage of nine miners stuck deep beneath the Western Pennsylvania earth, in a town less than an hour from Pittsburgh. We all watched it intently until my parents excused themselves for the hospital cafeteria, Grandpa's children not long after.

Loren smiled and nudged carefully next to me on my bed. I wrapped her hand in mine. She told me about her trip, about how frantically she'd ended it, I caught her up on matters obvious, and then a fine silence came over us. We were as alone as we could be: Grandpa now asleep, breathing heavy and low in the bed next to us. CNN field reporters were cloaked by the television's thin film of static, reporting that the Pennsylvania miners might still survive—that there might be enough breathable air beneath the surface—and I wanted so badly then to apologize to Loren, maybe for this moment and maybe every moment of the last six months, all of which felt like my fault, and much of it was—but she, stroking my knuckles with her fingertips, seemed uninterested in any such thing.

So I focused on other, more recent unfinished business.

"Do me a favor," I asked her. "Can you find my surgery scar?"

Loren moved to her feet, then peeked down into my hospital pajamas and squinted. I lifted myself up off of the bed as best I could, back arched, balls of my feet pinned to the base of the bed.

"Found it," she said.

"Is it on my ass?"

"Kind of on your hip?" she said.

"Back or front?"

"Front . . . *ish*," Loren said.

"*Front hip?*"

"Sorry, baby."

"Malpractice," I said, then rubbed my thumb and forefinger together. "Problems: *solved.*"

"Indeed," she said, then smiled and climbed back next to me, back onto her thin slice of hospital bed.

CH. 3

Q&A

Acromegaly is one of the world's oldest diseases, detected in skeletal remains dating back to the Neolithic era. The condition wasn't formally named until 1885, when French neurologist M. Pierre Marie had a hunch about two patients with headaches similar to my own. Early treatments for pituitary tumors ranged from medical marijuana to hormone therapy in the form of "animal extracts": fluid made from the spines, spleens, and thyroid glands of eagles, or from the pituitary glands of dead sheep (three spoonfuls a day), which yielded only intermittent success. Eventually doctors removed skull sections to relieve symptoms, a technique that proved only slightly more effective. "The patient is said to have been transformed," reported one doctor in 1898 who'd opened his subject's skull four inches, "'from being a miserable imbecile to a useful, intelligent being.'"

In 2002? Gum incisions and nose gauze. But even after more than a century the biggest challenge to an acromegaly diagnosis remained just that: diagnosing it. The condition carries with it such an idiosyncratic, disconnected menu of indicators that it's rare for a non-endocrine doctor to connect the dots: skin tags, hardened skin, fatigue, impaired vision, a deepened voice—things that rarely scream "brain tumor."

And it was in this way that Dr. Parsens and her team began to conduct a thorough recon of my body, checklisting the full gamut of symptoms. It began with three simple questions, and Parsens seemed, for the first time, concerned and almost loving when she asked them, hugging her clipboard to her chest, her voice transformed into something humane and light. My answers were all some version of the same thing, and Parsens didn't bother to write down any of them, I realized later, because she already knew what I'd say.

QUESTION ONE: "Are you having trouble sleeping?"

ANSWER: I hadn't enjoyed a civil night's rest in over a year, which isn't to say that my body didn't lobby for it. Each night throughout my last year of college in Pittsburgh, I lay worried on the mattress (no box spring) that lay on the floor of my room, the smallest in a five-bedroom, off-campus house I shared with kind, prodigy-like engineering majors who spent weekend afternoons building intricate catapults out of kitchenware. I started each night on my back, then on my side, then my back again until my eyelids finally pulled down. Any hint of sleep, though, triggered a sudden, ugly surge of airlessness through my bones. It gripped my throat then ran like a live current through my ribcage. It took less than a second, but it felt torrent-like, a vacuum pulling my ribs in hard toward my heart until I jerked myself awake with a nightmare gasp. It was unstoppable, metronomic. Every night it happened all night—*sleep, snap awake. Sleep, snap awake*—and the only antidote I found was to scrounge couch money for alcohol. A twelve-pack of canned beer, a fifth of rum, a Coke to chase—anything to push myself away to slumber as my mother often had, with solitary drunkenness.

My days became late-waking and irritated, napless and sore with hangovers. I ghosted through them, dreading nightfall, fearing the ticks of what seemed to be my body's new natural clock. Each night I sat alone in the living room well after my roommates had gone to bed, watching repeat loops of *The Box* and *Antiques Roadshow*—no cable for us—wondering if and when my chest bones might truly collapse and worse, if I'd be sober enough to wake myself to prevent it. The only nights I slept through were the ones spent next to Loren's warm body, her weekend flights to Pittsburgh somehow granting a thankful, mild reprieve.

So: "Yes," I told Dr. Parsens. "I have not been sleeping well."

QUESTION TWO: "Any joint or nerve pain?"

ANSWER: There had emerged, along with that impossible sleeplessness, a sharp, steady pain in what I discovered was my sciatic nerve. The pain ran from my right ass cheek down the back of my thigh, tightening my body like a strung bow. I hadn't pulled it or injured it. Like with the sleeplessness, it just appeared. Sitting in my three-hour writing workshops at school, on the hard chair at my computer desk—any long span turned me sore and bent, like a premature codger. I carried a rattling bottle of ibuprofen in my shoulder bag, popping two or three per hour throughout each day, which rarely worked. I spent my final days as an English major walking hunched and gingerly around my city campus, stopping to do back and leg stretches in the hallways outside of my classrooms, propped upright up against the wall holding each ankle for one-minute intervals as my classmates walked by, off-put and curious.

"Would you please see a goddamn *doctor*," my mother would say as I shuffled across the carpet of my parents' house on weekends—where I did my laundry, pilfered their fridge and, once they fell asleep, their wallets. Each time she said it, though, I'd wave her off. Until my mother's heart procedures, we weren't a family that was trigger-happy regarding doctor input. My parents owned a blue, hardbound medical encyclopedia, which they used at key moments in my youth to gauge and verify the seriousness of every potential illness: chicken pox, ingrown nails, and most embarrassingly at age fifteen, my first bout of jock itch—a shuddering, awful exam that happened first in our living room with my golden retriever curled at my feet, then in the stories my mother later told to relatives about my surprising "development" in that area. My parents checked symptoms against the text and sidebars of that blue book, and sought out home (or cheaply purchased) remedies before relenting to the flat-aired waiting room of our family doctor.

But my mother's procedures had sparked a new zealotry in her. She became a bloodhound for maladies. Any confession of a symptom or complaint of a bio-tic sent her into rapid diagnosis mode. My aunt's hairy mole? Melanoma. My uncle's stomach problems? Crohn's. And when it came to my sciatic pain (I did not tell her, or anyone, about the sleeplessness), she cursed me for my near lack of exercise—I'd recently dropped out of a one-credit "Physical Education" course because the leg and ass pain was so sharp and debilitating I couldn't touch my toes, let alone run laps—then she wore on me for weeks until finally I agreed to see a university-sanctioned physical therapist.

He moved my leg around, determined nothing, then scheduled me for biweekly sessions with another therapist at a large, intimidating sports medicine complex across town, a hub for Pittsburgh's rehabbing pro athletes. The new therapist uncovered as little as the first. When he noticed I was too tight to touch my toes, he put me on a regimen of "flexibility training." I sat on the edge of one of the many exam tables—planted across the floor of the training center like wide, cushioned pommel horses— merely lifting my right leg in the air and pointing my toes to the ceiling. Tables away, Penguins' defensemen and Steelers' linemen were lost in agony from the stress on their torn, mending bodies. For my "cool down," I lay on my stomach, flipping through used paperbacks of *Birds of America* and *Lolita* while an ice-filled garbage bag rested loosely across my sore rear end.

"It was useless," I told Dr. Parsens. "Nothing worked."

"Never does," she said.

LAST QUESTION: "So how about sweating? Have you been sweating far more than usual?"

ANSWER, IMMEDIATELY: "Dear god yes."

The sweats came on when everything else did, in the late spring of 2001. My college tenure moved, as I knew it would, from *five* to *five-point-five* years. I had a friend who'd reached a similar milestone, so one evening we met at a bar on the South Side of Pittsburgh to commiserate. We hadn't seen one another much in recent weeks. I'd been hiding under a cloud of frantic labor. I carried a full course load, made $6.50 an hour as a part-time fact-checker at a regional magazine, twice as much as a hotel-complex lifeguard, and freelanced in between, gorging myself on responsibility in my fifth year to somehow undo the itinerant bullshit of my first four. The night was temperate, the bar well ventilated. Within two sips of my first beer, though, thick beads of sweat appeared on my forearms, on the backs of my hands, and streamed into the wells of my eyes. My friend looked at me as if I were melting.

I'd been a moderate sweater for years—something I was silently proud of—but from then on the quick, heavy spells arrived a few times daily. I got them in overheated rooms or after hot showers, but mostly the sweats came without warning and with the cruel timing of adolescent erections. In classes, at parties, during interviews with local musicians for the upstart "happenings around town" website I wrote serviceable event profiles for. Midway through talking with a twangy, Bonnie Raitt–type after her set at a rib cook-off, I realized I'd ruined two pages of notes just by resting my hand on my notebook.

Toward the end of that summer I'd booked an interview with a tan, slow-talking neo-folk singer, a woman who'd gotten a rare dose of extra-Pittsburgh attention for her upcoming LP. I'd itched to turn the small Q&A I'd been assigned into something far meatier, a feature profile not just on the singer herself, but on "the plight of solo artists in a music-averse town" (I'd written the pitch before I even met the woman; it sat unfinished in an email I planned to send to my editor the next morning). I arrived early to the club where she was set to play a show to talk with her, pre-performance, like we'd arranged. But she arrived late, walked by, smiled and asked if we could do it post-show instead. It was hot in the club but not too hot—just the lovely, addictive heat of an excited crowd—yet I spent the next nine songs at the bar, ordering ice waters and waving a stack of her press materials in front of my face like a makeshift hand fan, trying and failing to ward away the sweats. It didn't work. By the time she'd finished her encore, signed merch, ducked backstage, then reemerged— her draped, flowered skirt exchanged for yoga pants, the sketch of modest make-up wiped clean from her face—I was soaked, dried off, then soaked again. Thick drops fell from my chin. My button-down stuck to my back, belly, chest and shoulders. Dark splotches bled though the front of my pant legs.

I asked the singer about her "influences," and she politely slid me a stack of cocktail napkins. I asked about her Pittsburgh roots and how they "informed her work," and she tilted her head with an awful kind of sympathy, asked if I wanted another ice water. I lobbed a compliment regarding my favorite track on the advance CD the singer's people had sent me—a neat, synthy number that had, when she played it that night, prompted a scattered, loving sing-along—and her face went flat. "Yeah," she said, "that's probably the most commercial thing on the LP," a flash of finger quotes around the word "commercial." I plugged along—*How do you think the new songs will translate to non-local markets? Do you think sites like Napster have helped to widen your appeal outside of the Greater Pittsburgh area?*—and her eyes went to my sweat-beaded forearms, then to the odd, damp circles along the tops of my thighs. It was no longer hot in the club. Everyone had left and taken their electricity with them, and the singer's answers rarely moved beyond the innocuous quotes in her press packet, a copy of which now sat on the bar, dampened and ink-bled as if it had been spilled upon, which, in a sense, it had been. When we finished talking I was terrified to offer her my sweat-soaked hand, so before the handshake I stood (slowly, barely upright, like someone's ailing grandfather) and dried it on the ass of my pants. She didn't offer her number for follow-up, and I no longer wanted it anyway. The pitch to my editor remained unsent and the Q&A ran as intended: online, lifeless and throwaway.

So what, then, did I think was happening? Metaphysical penance? During my trips to the physical therapist for my sciatic pain, I became fixated on an essay written by an author about her underachieving friend, a lazy, wannabe writer who was "resistant to forward motion" and died at twenty-two of a rare, mysterious hantavirus. He'd "accomplished nothing in his life other than his death," the writer wrote, and had been, according to her theory, plucked from the earth's surface due to unabashed obsolescence, proof of "some kind of devilish warden hovering over our lives, whispering in our waxy ears, 'Do something, or die.'" I'd aligned myself with some frantic resume-builders and seemed to be gaining traction as a semi-journalist, but the sweating, the sleeplessness, and the sciatic pain were all mutations of that theory, I thought. Warning shots. I felt like I was dissolving by the day, pulling apart in strange increments, and that the only way to cure it was to lash out in bold fits of production, make myself as employable as possible and flee Pittsburgh to hide away in the gray streets and buildings of New York City.

When I got there I slept somewhat better next to Loren, but the limping and sweating went nowhere. On crowded subway rides thin streams ran down my rail-hanging arm and dripped off my elbow, sometimes onto the heads and faces of shorter riders who'd carved out a space for themselves beneath my wingspan. Whatever professional momentum I'd built in Pittsburgh halted. By the time my tumor ruptured I'd had three actual job interviews in New York—editorial or publicity assistant jobs for obscure Manhattan companies—and for each I brought with me a fresh shirt to change into outside the building before signing in with the receptionist. But in the short time it took a hiring manager to greet me, arm extended, I was already soaked from the shoulders down, my handshake cold and slippery enough to dismiss immediately.

On the day my tumor ruptured, I left a backyard party in Brooklyn because I couldn't contain the flow of my own sweat. Loren had been gone for three days, and I'd grown sick of my own company, convinced myself to see real people, to "be social." My only option was a cookout hosted by the boyfriend of an acquaintance from high school whom I'll call Diane, someone who had, like me, moved from Pittsburgh to New York at the start of 2002. But unlike me she'd immediately found a job and friends and most recently a boyfriend, Tony, a Brooklyn-born pot dealer who lived a few subways stops from my apartment, in a row house with his mother and three sisters, all as wide-framed and heavy and pleasant as Tony himself. Like all of that July now seems in my memory, the heat that day was fog-like and oppressive, and though I made a nervous point not to run there or even walk fast, by the time I arrived at Tony's I was a mess of wet limbs. Socks run through with sweat, shirt and shorts heavy, darkened and conspicuous, droplets falling from the ends of my fingertips, the bend of my elbow.

Tony had an in-ground pool jammed into his narrow slice of fenced-in backyard, and clusters of people hovered around the grass in front of it, awaiting food from the smoking grill: loud laughs and cracked beers and interesting haircuts. I gravitated to the few I knew—Diane and two of her college friends, a schoolteacher and her filmmaking fiancé, both of whom I'd met weeks before at Angry Wade's. Within seconds of greeting me they wanted to get me paper towels, a seat. "You *okay*, dude?" they asked. "I'm *fine*," I said, then braced for the standard micronarratives of the run-in, where each person con-

denses *what they have* and *what they want* into short, positive arcs
to update at later run-ins; to report, without exclaiming: *Hey!
Look! I'm doing it!*

The schoolteacher wanted to escape a poisonous staff environment to work more meaningfully with "below-grade-level
readers." Her fiancé, happy with his day job at a production
company, was recruiting a PA team for an upcoming forty-
eight-hour filmmaking challenge. And Diane, who worked
reception at an art gallery located in a gentrifying enclave of
Brooklyn, just wanted to get high, or talk about getting high,
or reminisce about times in which she'd gotten high. I knew all
of this, and I readied myself to pretend to be excited about it,
then do my part, which was to let each person know, again, that
nothing had progressed in my own micronarrative, that I still
had no leads, that if anyone hears of anyone who needs an editor or a writer or a fact-checker, will you please let me know?

But that day I didn't allow myself the chance. Instead the
filmmaker and the schoolteacher looked at my soaked body
and asked things like "Look: Are you sure you're okay?" And
though I assured everyone as I always did that yes, I was fine,
Diane's face turned urgent. "I'll get you some water," she said,
then returned with Tony the pot dealer, who was holding a roll
of paper towels. Diane handed me the water, Tony the paper
towels. He opened a folding chair and slapped it.

"Take a quick seat, man," he said, so I did, laughing as if to
say, *Look: I have no clue what's happening here*, which was true. For
the next twenty minutes I sat on that chair patting my face and
arms with fistfuls of paper towels, smiling politely to anyone

who met my eye, watching droplets hit the dry red brick below me. The sweats were usually short: ten-minute bursts that faded as quickly as they came. But this one kept steady, and as the concerned people fell back into their conversations, I slipped away, walked slowly back to the F train, then back into my apartment, while my pores gushed.

CH. 4

THE BIG WHATEVER

Other symptoms of acromegaly/growth hormone secretions, along with my own experience of them in the months leading to my rupture, are as follows:

Tiredness, fatigue, depression (yep)
Hypertension (nope)
Polyps on the colon/cancer of the colon (thankfully, no)
Lapsed menstrual cycle (n/a)

But GH overflow's main indicator, and what leads to most diagnoses, is how it fundamentally shifts one's bone structure. For those who abuse GH (certain pro athletes, bodybuilders) the change is often fast, brash, and cartoonlike: a widened jaw, caved-in temples, a protruding, Cro-Magnon brow. But

Dr. Parsens said the level of GH secretions produced by a pituitary tumor trickle into the bloodstream in the tiniest of increments. Unlike with GH abusers, there's no great spike in musculature. The concave temples and shelflike brow, the hardening of the skin and widening of the feet and hands—acromegaly is Greek for *great extremities*—all of that still occurs. But those changes happen slowly, Parsens said, with a stealth that can sneak by the everyday eye for years, even decades.

"We mostly catch it in middle-aged patients who switch over to a new doctor," was how Parsens put it to me in 2002. "Someone with no visual history with the patient's features."

She asked me for pictures of myself over a span of five years. All I had was a university ID and an expired Pennsylvania driver's license. Parsens held them up to my ears as if comparing wallpaper swatches.

"See the temples?" she said to her team.

"Mmm-hmm," one said.

"Hands," said another.

I kept still, like an inspected show-dog. I looked to my mother, who'd leaned into my father's ear, whispering. Loren and I met eyes from her seat by my bed. One young specialist unsheathed a large hoop with metal ringlets on it, which she slipped on my fingers, noting each measurement. Another pressed and kneaded at my feet, and a third—a timid woman who had not, to that point, looked me in the eye—moved her face close to mine, her eyes scanning from my temples to my forehead, then back to her clipboard as she took notes.

I was struck with the urge to call for a mirror, but it wouldn't have mattered. I would have seen only a face painted with left-over surgery blood, nostrils wide as a bull's, nothing that looked like the face I knew. I decided instead to let the crew gauge and describe my shape to one another, taking mental notes of their new discoveries to follow up on later: *the hands have meat to them . . . bunions, malformation on the toes . . . bow-like forearms, wrists.*

Somewhere around the time Dr. Parsens said, "Tongue out," then pinched in lightly with a set of metal calipers—apparently acromegalics were thick-tongued—my mother broke away from her mumbled conversation with my father and raised her hand like a child in class.

"*I* saw it," she said. "Two weeks ago. *I* saw it."

Two weeks ago had been Independence Day, and I'd taken a seventy-eight-dollar Greyhound across Pennsylvania to celebrate it with my extended family, a pack of second- and third-generation Italians whose knowledge of Italy was lim-ited to overwrought pronunciation (*rig-GOAT, capa-COAL*) and cured-meat-laden summer gatherings at my grandfather's lakeside cabin on the banks of Indian Lake, an hour south of Pittsburgh. When I got there, my mother was alarmed by how I looked. It was the first she'd seen me since I'd moved to New York. She followed me throughout the afternoon, iced glass of Pinot in hand, her eyes squinted, inspecting my shape with the relentless suspicion of a drug-sniffing dog. She reported her findings first to me, then to whoever stood closest.

"I don't like the way you *look*," she said. Then to my father: "I don't like the way he *looks*."

Or: "Did you lose weight in your face?" Then to my aunt: "He looks like he lost weight in his face."

Or: "You just look *off* . . ."

My brother was sitting on the deck of the lake house trying badly to sneak a beer, holding it under a tabletop. He was wiry and young-looking even for eighteen, the neck ring of his T-shirt hanging off the back of his head like a nun's habit. I tried to give him advice about his first semester in college—a small university in the Midwest he'd received a soccer scholarship to attend.

"Just go to class," I said. "Even if you don't want to."

"Got it," he said. "So do the *exact opposite of Mike*."

The rest of my family greeted me as expected. Aside from my aunt C., a nomadic textbook author and interior designer, I was the only other Scalise who'd had a graduation ceremony beyond high school. Everyone before me had either failed out of college, made faulty investments, or made some other grand miscalculation of youth that triggered my grandfather, the heating and air-conditioning company's founder, to sweep in and absorb them into the business, providing them with houses, cars, management-level incomes.

In return they lived in a state of indentured gratitude, beholden to him as father and supervisor, and now, in his retirement, to the cache of demeaning, chore-like demands he dispatched, for which no one had earned the footing to say *no*. At all hours of the night, he tapped his sons to be strongmen for the late-paying tenants in the shabby apartments he'd acquired just outside of Pittsburgh to keep busy during pension years. He often summoned my father or uncles to his home to execute his petty bank and property transactions, like balance transfers and bill mailings. The previous Thanksgiving I'd watched my father, a reserved, imposing man of forty-eight, the oldest of his siblings, reduced to a petulant fury of clenched fists and wall punches at my grandfather's strict orders that he, at 4:00 P.M., immediately find and purchase a fully baked and seasoned turkey to replace the one my grandmother had deemed, in a spell of disgust, "unservable."

His brothers, my uncles, responded to news of my graduation plans by slipping me hunks of money, then telling me what a mistake I was making with it. Six months later at the lake house, after that money was gone, the sight of me sent them into self-pleased, cliché monologues about New York City's failures. Standard of living, job climate, Al Qaeda magnet, whatever. I had arguments to the contrary, good ones, but zero credibility, so I said nothing. They called me "Mr. Brooklyn" and "City Boy," or simply shouted out the location when they walked past me—"NEW YORK!"—as if the five boroughs were mine now, a place I was *of*.

That night people gathered eagerly and earnestly around the lake to light tiny bonfires, or set out on their pontoons to watch the sparkling remains of every crack and boom fall to the lake's surface. My family sat on the deck in sorted piles: my uncles and aunts with their children slung across their laps, my grandparents at one table, me and my brother at another with my parents, who took turns blowing folds of cigarette smoke out into the air.

On my way to bed that night, my mother appeared in the hallway with a full glass of wine, looking severe and unmovable, as if she'd caught me up to something. She pointed at my head, traced her finger around it slowly, and said:

"Your. Face. Does. Not. Look. Right."

Then, after a few wordless seconds:

"C'mere. Gimme a hug."

Two weeks later, turns out she was dead-on. But my mother wasn't smug in the brain trauma ward, or self-satisfied. She sounded perplexed and guilty, a confusion not unlike what I'd seen during those maddening talks following her mother's death years before.

"*I* saw it," she said, shaking her head, as though she could have stopped anything, as though the tumor wasn't already crawling on my pituitary that July Fourth, well into an indelible campaign on my shape that neither I nor my father nor Loren ever noticed. Not once.

During my six years as a lifeguard I made thirty-two saves, all of which I remember with the clarity and retro-vision that one might a wedding or a maiden skydive. A toddler sneaks out of her mother's eyesight and into the deep end of the pool. A long-haired thirtysomething, trying to recapture the lost reverse-gainer of his youth, slips on the diving board and splits wide the skin on his shin. A plump deaf woman jumps feet-first into the shallow end then yelps high and awful like a homesick puppy, her feet striking the pool floor so hard that the force of it wiggles through her aging bones and re-dislocates her shoulder. Then time breathes slowly. The air stills. And I stand up from my perch above them, sound a long whistle, then launch, as if pulled from the moment itself, watching it as it happens. *I got you, I got you*, I say as I hook my arm around them, people lined like spectators along the pool deck watching as I deliver each person to a very public kind of safety.

Maybe it was the salve of information—finally knowing what was wrong, what had truly been tearing away at me all this time, even if I didn't understand it—but I felt that same sharpness and calm the night after my operation. An absence of anxiety. A disassociation. A slowness. Dr. Parsens finished her exams, promised more in the days to come, then left with her team. Loren and my parents soon did the same, leaving only myself and Grandpa in the hospital room—he cavorting, yelling out nonsense to the quickly darkening air. Me: flat on the bed, spinal fluid piling up in my back, leaking from my nose. I watched more CNN, more of the Pennsylvania miners—rescue drilling began the next morning, the outcome still quite hopeful—but shut it off after the third or fourth loop through the news cycle and sat quiet with the flooding mental loop of my own news, frightened but enthralled.

I would have probably been able to sleep, too—my first true night of sleep in over a year—but after lights-out Grandpa grew untethered and paranoid, unhooking himself from his machines just as quickly as the nursing crew re-hooked him, calling out to me ceaselessly as if I were the son he couldn't recognize during the day. He said the same thing all night, hours upon hours of this anti-lullaby, which I listened to because there was no other choice:

"Joey. *Joey*," he said. "I can't seem to find . . . a suitable way . . . to get out of this *chair*."

And because there was now time, and because they needed to fill it with something, for the next four days my parents took morning trips around the city, Loren their makeshift guide. It was their first trip to New York, and they rounded Manhattan on the Staten Island Ferry, went to Ground Zero and Little Italy, then brought me leftovers from their meals: penne alla vodka and pepperoni slices which, after lunches and dinners of hospital blandness, I gladly maneuvered past my stitch-bound gumline.

Four days in, the leaking spinal fluid was now a faint, random trickle, nearly unnoticeable. Aside from the lagging refuse of dry blood—which still, after many washes, peeled from the sides of my face in tough, jerky-like strands—convalescence felt relaxing, pleasant. At the same time I itched to break free, to move headlong into the big whatever.

That same shift happened to Loren and my parents. They'd adjusted to the offset urgency of the episode, unsure how to manage the unwelcome gusts that blew in from their outside lives. My father—our most experienced spectator of illness— became increasingly irritated with the calls from his brothers/ coworkers in Pittsburgh, each asking when he'd "finally be done in New York." He talked about my Brooklyn neighborhood as though he was actually vacationing there. It became, for him, a reprieve. "Your mother and I went to that bakery on your corner this morning," he'd say. "It's great. So close to the apartment." "Your downstairs neighbor gave us his parking space last night. Frank," he'd tell me, then nod to himself. "Nice guy."

My mother swung between decompression and aggravation. One afternoon we'd play a series of tension-free games of Scrabble (all of which she won, hands down). Then I'd hear from my father about how she'd snapped at Loren for ducking out to de-stress over a beer with a friend, or how she'd slipped into tears while leaving yet another ignored voicemail for her sister in Jersey, all of which kept her rifling nightly through packs of Marlboro Lights at the table by the back window of my apartment.

Occupying them all became an increasingly crucial task. Each afternoon before their arrival I'd prepare updates on several statuses: (a) that of the trapped Pennsylvania miners (Escaped! Unharmed!), (b) the manner in which Grandpa had driven me sleepless the night previous (the same every night: "Joey, *Joey*—"), and finally (c) that of the latest tests from Dr. Parsens and her team.

There were few early or easy answers. Pinpointing where acromegaly ended and hormonal barrenness began was a complicated effort, it seemed, one that sparked Parsens's team with an off-putting excitement they tried hard, and failed, to conceal. Parsens and her crew spent those days conducting *more* quizzes about how much I went to the bathroom, ate, exercised, and had sex in the months leading up to the tumor's rupture; *more* fumbling measurements of my body parts: the length and circumference of my arms, the size and shape of my testicles. For that last exam one of Parsens's crew—the same reticent woman who wouldn't look me in the eyes—appeared alone, extended the dull, cold tip of her index finger to them for a few seconds, almost like pressing an elevator button, then said, "Looks good," and walked briskly from the room.

On my last day in the Upper Manhattan brain trauma ward Parsens handed me her business card along with another, more serious-looking card for DR. ANNE V. WALLA, CLINICAL DIRECTOR, NEUROENDOCRINE UNIT. She told me there was far more monitoring and adjusting to be done, and that I should put myself under the new doctor's care "as soon as is feasible."

"Fine work, doctor," I told her in a deep, silly voice, then she smiled and handed me prescriptions, each small slip of paper a brick in the foundation of my new hormonal makeup.

Avis was, sadly, off duty my last afternoon, so once the nursing crew took a set of forceps and unspooled ribbons of bloody gauze from my nostrils like a circus clown's endless handkerchief, I wrote THANK YOU AVIS! on the dry-erase board on the wall, then drew an ill-proportioned two-door sedan right beneath it. Loren packed my clothes, gifts cards, and stationery from Jean the VFT tech into a backpack, along with some fresh pairs of hospital pajamas that I'd sweet-talked the staff into stealing for me. Grandpa's children and my parents had become confidantes of a sort—bound, perhaps, by the intimacy of their shared helplessness—and they all shook hands and said, "Good luck" and "You take care."

Before the orderlies loaded my weak bones onto a wheelchair, I tried to nudge Grandpa—Joe, I found out, his name was Joe—to say a nice goodbye, but he was wrapped up in his bedsheets, sleeping at last, his breath beating at a slow wheeze.

Two hours later we were getting sushi in Brooklyn. Why not? The place was small and wood-paneled, and my mother giggled as slices of tuna fell from the iffy grip of her chopsticks and splashed into the well of soy sauce on the table. My father talked about the many ways he'd seen chefs prepare rolls on the PBS cooking shows he watched every Sunday. I talked obnoxiously about how the city buildings in Pittsburgh seemed *so small now* in my memory. Loren sat mostly silent, her hand on mine, her fingers tracing my knuckles, her hands tan and warm after most of a week on the West Coast, mine like the rest of me: white and cold from the hospital fluorescents.

The insurance arrangement through my family's company was only eight days old, which meant I had no insurance cards, so after lunch my mother returned with Loren to my apartment, and my father agreed to go with me to the pharmacy a few blocks away to cover the costs for the first pack of medications I'd take from here on out: Hydrocortisol, Synthroid, AndroGel, desmopressin. The streets were loud and cramped for a weekday afternoon, and I was weak and disoriented as I walked on them. My legs felt like empty straws. My father tugged at my arm as I shuffled loosely behind him at the crosswalks, and I felt the heat bounce off the concrete onto my shins. We made our way through the blocks, weaving around oncoming walkers. I held my palm up in front of my face, squinted hard through the sunlight, trying to point out to my father my favorite parts of the neighborhood. The offtrack betting place on the corner. The two-dollar beer garden by the subway station. Angry Wade's. It was what my life looked like now, and I wanted so badly to show it to him, but I could barely even see it myself.

My parents left for Pittsburgh, then Loren for her shift at the bakery, and I was alone for the first time with my new, hormoneless body, excited and scared, unsure what to do with it. (Watch TV? Check email?) I sifted through the backpack Loren brought from the brain trauma ward, put on a fresh, soft pair of hospital pajama pants, then sat on the couch with the business card Dr. Parsens had given me for ANNE V. WALLA, CLINICAL DIRECTOR, NEUROENDOCRINE UNIT. I picked up the phone and dialed.

"Dr. Walla isn't taking on patients at this time, sir."

"Oh," I said, "I was told to call."

"Dr. Walla *isn't taking on patients at this time*—"

Then with a sharp, sudden disgust that shocked me, I hung up, dropped the phone on the floor, its plastic backflap cracking open, spilling AA batteries onto the hardwood. My hands shook. My teeth gritted. In no time I was pacing through my apartment, a fountain of profanity. I found Dr. Parsens's card and dialed her number, then left a long, acid voicemail that I regretted in real time, one heavy with entitlement and self-pity—"I did *exactly what you said*"—that channeled every sentiment I hadn't been able to convey to all the stale-grinned hiring managers who wished me well at the end of those terrible job interviews, then passed me over, as Dr. Anne V. Walla's assistant just had, with pure disinterest.

It was not a call Dr. Parsens should have felt compelled to return.

I heard from her within the hour.

"Give me five minutes," Parsens said.

Then, five minutes later:

"Sir, this is Dr. Walla's office. How does next week sound?"

PART TWO

CH. 5

IN THE EVENT OF SOMETHING UNHOLY

The biggest mistake people make when crafting a mass email, disaster-themed or otherwise, is assuming anyone wants to read the thing. Good mass emails delicately handle at least two social dangers. The first is encroachment: inflicting your experience upon a friend's unsuspecting inbox (e.g., the birth or growth of someone's children, a humbling tour in the Peace Corps). The second? Activating the implied contract of the mass email, in which someone is burdened with pressure to reply to it, or worse, decide not to, which of course is a reply in itself.

Addressing those dangers up front can work in a mass email's favor, particularly when it comes to catastrophes. I sent mine the evening I got out of the brain trauma ward, and it was, like so many other mass emails, unwieldy, imposing, and obnoxious.

It covered my stay in every hospital, plus every diagnosis detail and supporting character as they'd revealed themselves along the way.

There were numbered sections. Eight of them.

My email's saving grace, though, may have been this early sentence, which I can only assume triggered people to respond as thoughtfully and earnestly as they did: "I know that most of these unsolicited updates are often viewed as assumptive, so I figured I would go through my address book and click on everyone who I would like to receive unsolicited information about and send this email to them (them is you)."

Is it a transparent, ingratiating move? Yes. But it's also an important one; one that showcases the mass email's most unsung advantage over the forms of large-scale e-sharing that have emerged in the years since my tumor ruptured: metered, indirect intimacy. A handwritten letter can seem in this context almost *too* personal, a blog post or status update too homogenous. I wrote thank-you cards to every person who sent me things or contacted me in the hospital ("I can't begin to tell you how thankful Loren and I are for your support during this strange and confusing time . . .") but the mass email, I figured, could work as a back channel to a handpicked quorum of folks with whom I hoped to share the *true* experience: childhood friends, mentors, people whom adulthood had been pulling me slowly away from. *This happened,* I wanted to say, *and I'd love to gather you all in the same well-lit room and tell you about it. But I can't, so here's an email, because I miss you all and want to hear from you.* Then I did, and it was nice.

But my mass email was also—and this, again, is a fantastic trait of the medium—a retaliation against the not-so-close people who'd come to decorate my life in recent years, who, unlike me, had done things on time and with promise. For the last year and a half they'd sent me these types of emails detailing their exciting jobs in marketing and their trips to distant lands, about their internships and entry-level victories and houses with yards. I shared my brain tumor story with all of them. The newly midmanagement finance officer who'd once borrowed my Honda, wrecked it, then wouldn't pay for repairs. The competitive, snark-addled group of writer-types in Pittsburgh, with whom I'd once worked on a lazy rip-off of a better, funnier, more ironic literary magazine. The person from my first college in Ohio who *actually faked graduating*, who was far short credit-wise (I'm talking years) yet at the four-year point simply bought a cap and gown like everyone else, brought his family to a ceremony, sat through it without incident, and then *got a job before me*—I put all of those people in the address line, too.

My brain tumor, my acromegaly, my hormonelessness—it was bigger news than all of their news combined. And the news was horrible, ill-defined and raw, featuring opinions about catheters and spinal tap strategies and descriptions of bloody nostril gauze. But it was *mine*, a truly adult happening I could lay claim to, and I was—there's no other way to put this—far too proud of the achievement to keep it to myself.

It was in that complicated spirit that just days after I sent that email, shoved back into the world with a functionless pituitary gland, I thought it a good idea to fly to Ohio to be in a' wedding. I was a groomsman for Mark McKiernan, one of the few friends that I still cared about from my Ohio days, and I was determined to fulfill the commitment. I was also the only one who thought this was a good idea. *Cancel and rest*, my doctors said. *Let your blood flow adjust to the new medicines.* Loren and my family felt similarly. Even McKiernan told me not to come. I'd been a late addition after all, a replacement for a groomsman who'd already dropped out, the first alternate to the last man on the pew, and throughout my recovery it was made politely clear by Mark, his parents and his fiancée that yes, they wished me well, but the event wouldn't suffer greatly (or at all) without me.

Of course I ignored them. Of course I phoned airlines from my hospital bed and rescheduled my flights at zero cost ("But I'm *in the hospital*—"), insisted to Loren while I healed at home that I was "fine," that I felt a bit fatigued, but not so much that I couldn't bear a flight to Ohio, a seat in a church pew.

Loren and I attacked the rehearsal dinner in a cheery tandem. The dinner was at the bride's mother's house in suburban Youngstown the night we arrived, steel-legged bingo tables spread like linked dominos throughout the backyard. Loren and I wove our way among them, waving, saying hello, holding one another's hands, a slight squeeze on the other's fingertips when it was time to move on to the next person we barely knew. The details of my mass email had been passed along to many of the rehearsal guests in spotty, dubbed-tape ways. It was a telephone game of illness, where the only word anyone remembered was *tumor*, which meant that those who'd caught wind approached Loren and me with the meekness that one might a friend's just-widowed parent.

"Heyyyyyyyy."

"How *are* you?"

"You ok, dude?"

I told everyone I hadn't taken a shit in almost two weeks. The orderlies at the Upper Manhattan hospital had warned me on Day 9 that the pain medications they'd been feeding my veins all week were laced with by-products that kept me constipated—which had been the case since I walked into the ER over a week before—and that it would likely be that way for "just a bit longer."

"How much longer?" I'd asked.

"A day?" the orderly had told me. "Maybe two?"

Yet I arrived in Ohio on Day 12, three days after I left the hospital, without so much as a promising stomach churn. I'd eaten bran, drank coffee, smoked cigarettes: nothing. When people asked how I felt (hand on my arm, forced tone) I said, "Great! Haven't shit in two weeks!" Earlier, at the church run-through, I'd haggled openly with the wedding planner—a rigid, over-perfumed woman in a white blazer—to be positioned with a direct line to the restroom in the event of "something unholy."

Throughout the rehearsal dinner I asked why there weren't baked beans served, then before leaving for the evening, I pledged to a large swath of people—Mark and his fiancée included—that I'd wear adult undergarments beneath my tux just in case the stalemate ended, abruptly, midceremony.

"Formal Depends," I called them.

To say that I don't have hormones is just the easiest, most small-talk-ready way to say that my brain now lacks the ability to tell my glands to make them. A healthy pituitary gland, depending on how it interprets your needs, sends gusts of either stimulating or regulatory hormones to your body's glands—thyroid, adrenal, pineal—which get to work brewing and serving to the bloodstream the hormones necessary at any given time.

In the case of a typical pituitary tumor, the endocrine system usually falls back into step once the tumor is removed. But since mine ruptured, it destroyed my pituitary gland's ability to function. The other glands in my endocrine system—the ones that regulate the hormone flow that controls metabolism, hair growth (and loss), sleep, hunger, anxiety, and more—now lie in deep hibernation, waiting for an alarm clock that will never ring.

I can't report accurately what happened the morning after we arrived in Ohio, which hormone glands couldn't be woken. I can guess that my body was probably starved of either adreno-corticotropic or thyroid-stimulating hormone, both of which replenish harmful deficits of blood sugar, combat fatigue, and affect recovery speed. All I can say for certain was that at 7:00 A.M. on the day of the wedding, I was internally fucked. I lay on my back in the hotel bed, alarm pulsing, my arms pulled down by a soupy gravity. My hands and feet had lost sensation. My legs, chest, and back surged with deep aches and the skin on my face felt heavy, the air in my lungs sharp and jagged. During my first days out of the hospital I felt atrophied but otherwise fine. I'd ridden into Ohio on what felt like a tide pull of adrenaline. But now that energy was gone, replaced by something foreign and scraped out, limp but heavy.

Loren sat up in bed, put her hand on my arm.

"I'm going to try to stand up," I said.

"Don't."

"Tee time's in twenty minutes."

McKiernan had arranged a round of eighteen holes for the groomsmen.

"You don't even like golf," she said, which was true.

"This is true," I said, then pushed myself upward anyway, arms and legs slushy with a weight I hadn't felt before. It was just a matter of exhaustion, I thought, a pause before a second wind. But by the third hole I lacked the juice to even walk, so instead I chauffeured the rest of the crew, weaving across fairways and playing golf cart polo with shag balls in the rough. I hoped the sun on my skin might fuel me somehow. At lunch I sipped coffee, ate fruit, drank soda, anything to get my energy back, to reconjure the previous day's sharpness. But for the back nine holes, and for the rest of the day, and throughout the wedding ceremony, I walked upstream with a head ten pounds heavier, my limbs awkward as they failed to resume a light, familiar rhythm. I'd tried napping that afternoon—Loren beside me, brushing the hair by my ear—but the dogged, thorough nag of exhaustion turned me aggravated and restless.

I wore no Formal Depends beneath my tux pants that evening, because there was no progress in that regard. There was no progress in any regard. When the church organ blasted its high note, and we groomsmen filed to the front pew, I could barely lift my feet above a drag. I caught one on a pew leg and fell face-first into the oak seat. Groomsmen chuckled as they helped me back up.

McKiernan and his bride said and did all the things we'd rehearsed the night before. Mark, surprisingly, let out a tear during the vows. It was a fine, respectful ceremony and I might have been touched if I'd been able to see it through the previous day's eyes. But I could only concentrate on the vibrant soreness moving through my hands, knees, and chin, humming through my bones like a struck tuning fork. I could only muster long, pitiful stares ahead, an occasional soft clap, a late snicker at the pastor's tepid jokes.

After the ceremony a limousine drove the wedding party to a photographer's backyard, a lush, fenced-in array of ponds and tiny bridges and warm floral arrangements. The groomsmen and bridesmaids—people who, for the most part, I'd exchanged four-years-prior dorm room chats with and little else—had by now stopped asking me if I was OK, which meant I could finally stop telling them yes. I said very little during that ride, and no one—including Mark and his new wife—said much to me. I felt suspect and unwelcome now, and when I struggled to exit the limo later, I heard someone hiss, "*Jesus.*"

Mark had guessed on my tuxedo measurements during my hospital stay, and as a result my shoes were a half-size too small, the shirtsleeves several inches too long, the cummerbund snug as a girdle. By then I'd given up readjusting it, and let it crawl up my chest, a loose flap of white shirt hanging below it like an unoccupied pouch. It was late evening now, but still sunny and humid, and the photographer asked me more than once to tuck myself in. When I couldn't concentrate enough to make that happen, he laughed, shook his head, placed both hands on me and moved me between the shoulders of two groomsmen in the back row. I pulled my face into what I thought was a smile.

I saw that photo the next summer while back in Ohio for another wedding with most of the same people. In it, the wedding party is tan and plump and sedate. Mark and his wife look like brides and grooms do. The only visible part of me is my dewy, colorless head, a grimacing pale fleck trying hard to stay afloat amidst a grinning sea of bronze.

For weeks afterward I treated the trip as an act of courageous defiance. When I mentioned it to people and they asked, *Why didn't you just stay home?*, I wrapped my reasons in brave-sounding platitudes. "I figured I'd have the rest of my life to have doctors tell me what I can and can't do," I said. "What other option did I have: sit at home feeling sorry for myself?"

Non-self-pity, I told them, included a wedding reception. As night fell on Mark McKiernan's, I'd gotten some of my energy back but not much, so Loren and I stayed only for what we were obligated to: the cake-in-the-face moment; a bridesmaid crying and then vomiting on the pathway between the reception door and the limo. Then, on Day 13, at roughly 10:00 P.M., I finally felt a familiar pull in my gut. The next few hours on the hotel bathroom toilet seat were long and awful and more akin to childbearing than seems proper to describe. Loren sat on the bed outside the bathroom, talking to me, asking if I needed anything, but I stayed up longer than she could keep her eyes open.

The next morning we stood at the doorway of the hotel bathroom, silent and shame-faced behind a troubled hotel maintenance crew—two short men and one blonde, nonplussed woman—who each took turns slamming at that poor, beaten toilet with a plunger that looked like a rubber accordion on a stick.

"It just took a little bit . . . *longer* than usual for me to 'process the event,' if you know what I mean," was the line I later used to explain myself.

"That," Loren always made sure to note, "or you don't fucking listen."

CH. 6

A FEW SIMPLE REPAIRS

D r. Anne V. Walla's office was on the top floor in the neuroendocrine unit of the Upper Manhattan hospital, an exam room with little more than a plastic cross section of a brain on her desk and a dented AC unit that sputtered drops off the windowsill. She was wide-faced and polite, and kicked off the meeting with a series of questions: *Are you sleeping well? Are you going to the bathroom regularly? How's your energy? Are you perspiring regularly? Any pains? Where? How about headaches? Where? Follow my finger. Can you see it here? Here?*

My answers were as banal as possible. She wrote them down with purpose. Acromegaly's symptoms had disappeared en masse in the wake of my operation. My sciatic pain: gone. Sleep: sound. Sweating: reduced to a level befitting the heat of the season. As thankful as I was for it, the novelty of my body's return to normalcy and comfort had worn off after a day or two.

But not to Dr. Walla. I mentioned that I'd had a headache the previous day, just a light one, likely from caffeine, but that triggered her to ask a subset of questions about the location of the headache, its duration, what time of day it happened, if it was a sharp pain, a stabbing pain, if it felt focused or fog-like. Every crick in my neck, every tweak in the routine was grossly important.

We liked one another. Or at least I think we did. Walla wasn't a natural patient-care doctor. She was a study-and-publish hound, and I sensed early on that her patient load was scarce, that the few cases she did have were complex and strange. Our conversations were stuttered and rhythmless and interesting to navigate. What qualified in the outside world as small talk sparked in her a deep-seeming empathy.

"No, Loren and I aren't married," I told her during that first meeting. "Just living together."

"Oh *no*," she said. "I am *so, so* sorry about that."

I kept quiet about Mark McKiernan's wedding earlier that week, the numbing and the bottoming out. I knew I'd crossed some hormonal line. But it had been several days and nothing like it had happened again, so I'd ruled the episode a product of fresh medications mingling badly with old habits, confident that my bloodstream would grow more capable, my sense of those capabilities more acutely trained.

And besides: Dr. Walla and I were here to talk about the future. Our first job in these early months, she said, was to complete the task my neurosurgeons had started. My surgeon, fearing irreparable damage to my carotid—the artery that delivers oxygenated blood to the brain and eyes—had left behind a sliver of pituitary growth that had bumped up against it. Dr. Walla called it "residual tumor."

She said we had to determine what, if any, effect it had on my endocrine makeup, and if it might grow back, then set up a system by which we could track signs of regrowth. The tumor found strength in regeneration. If it grew back, it could return much stronger, and expand faster, and wreak much more damage on my body than the first one had. That would mean more bloodwork and dosage shifts, more consults with my neurosurgeons.

In the meantime we needed to gauge how much excess growth hormone had already insinuated itself into my bones and bloodstream. For this, Walla wanted tests. Many of them. Her assistant, Errol, a med student with a nervous, quiet laugh, came into the office and drew more blood. As he wrapped my bicep snug in a rubber ribbon and stabbed away at my forearm, looking for a good vein—I'd learned in the brain trauma ward that I was what the nurses liked to call a "hard stick"—Dr. Walla primed me with contact info for techs and specialists I'd need to see in the coming weeks and months.

"Go to this place for a heart ultrasound."

(GH overflow hardens the arteries.)

"Get your bone density exam here."

(GH overflow triggers and accelerates osteoporosis.)

"Errol, how about this date for the stress test?"

(—to test heart, thyroid, and adrenal response "under duress," which, following Mark McKiernan's wedding, I'd become quite curious about.)

"Sure thing," said Errol, filling a test tube with my blood, uncapping an empty one, replacing it.

"And I can afford to pay for all this?" I asked. I hadn't yet researched the geographic restrictions of the bogus insurance coverage through my family's heating and air-conditioning firm. The only discussion I'd had about the insurance plan at all took place via the bedside telephone in the Brooklyn training hospital, where I'd tried to explain to my father's office assistant that my brain was apoplectic, at full bleed, that all her helpful words were being rendered absolute nonsense to me the very moment she spoke them.

"Weird insurance," I told Dr. Walla.

Blood from my arm spat into one final test tube.

"Oh," she said. "Just tell these places it's for *my* office. And if you run into problems with copays or whatever, let me know. We'll sidestep it."

Walla told me to switch over to the new dosages at once. We scheduled another meeting for the following month, and Walla told me to call if anything was awry: if I couldn't sleep, or my vision clouded, or—god forbid—the sweats returned. Errol wrote his email address on a sheet of paper and said something similar. Then we were all standing in that drab office shaking hands like we'd struck some kind of merger—*I'm proud to be your new multi-fraction, your kid with no hormones*—smiling widely at one another, maybe even meaning it.

It was 1:00 A.M. and the woman in the kitchen was talking about her documentary-in-progress, a short, vérité profile of a female illusionist living in the wooded guts of Appalachia. I think I was a little scared of her. She was loud but fun-sounding and passionate, with a long black skirt and short, curly hair, empty beer cup held out to her side, twisting it slowly in her wrist like a searchlight as she self-assessed her film's main hurdle, which was this: the Appalachian illusionist was, the woman thought, "a good *character*," but after hours of filming she wasn't proving herself "a good protagonist." She didn't "want anything." The woman said this several times, but not in a way that invited advice—she seemed content to *have* the problem, not fix it—which left Ethan and me with little recourse but to nod and say meaningless things like "Ah, that sucks" and "It'll work itself out."

It was, after all, her birthday party, held at her walk-up in Greenpoint, and Loren and I had come as guests of Ethan, her coworker, whom we both knew from high school. Ethan had moved to New York from Pittsburgh two years before I did, after which he'd turned himself into a reactionary NYC connoisseur. Upon my arrival, Ethan was as giddy to share what he'd found there as I was to hear about it. "You can get anything delivered to you," he told me. "You want pot? Right to your door. Lobster? Here's the number." Our friendship, though, gravitated back to our origins. We spent evenings at his Lower East Side apartment watching cult films like *Donnie*

Darko and *Brother from Another Planet,* him pulling on a one-hitter, me with a beer, talking like spurned expatriates about the failures of Pittsburgh—or, more accurately, the ways in which Pittsburgh had failed *us.* Our high school was at the heart of an atrophied town a few miles outside of the city. It had been driven barren by industrial obsolescence, surrounded by soot-charred skeletons of once-chugging steel mills. Ethan and I had occupied similar positions during high school: art-geeks moving upstream against a steady flow of tough-minded teens, many of them products of mill-era holdovers waiting for an upswing that would never come. We'd both wanted distance from that experience. And now that we had it, where we came from was all we could talk about. We cataloged the stories of our shared acquaintances from back home, some of whom had already died—overdoses in public bathrooms, 3:00 A.M. car collisions followed by toxicology reports. But even if they hadn't died yet, we smugly turned them into apparitions anyway, failed souls lost to the graveyard in which they (and we) were born.

Ethan was generous with the fruits of his professional life, or at least what he'd made of it by then. He'd built a documentary editing career with no help from anyone already established in his field. He couch-surfed until he caught on at a film production company, then slept on the trampled-upon floors of Port Authority or Penn and Grand Central Stations until he could afford a deposit for his own place. "What you have to do," he told me about sleeping on those Penn Station nights, "is use your bag and coat as a mattress and always sleep face-up so

no one steals your shit. Having a knife on you also won't hurt."
I was as envious of him as I was inspired. Within two years he'd
found a good job editing clips at a tiny but well-known moviemaking house where he'd made moviemaking friends.

When I returned from the wedding in Ohio, Ethan called
to see how I was doing, which was when I learned about
his coworker's birthday party in Greenpoint. I was sore and
embarrassed from the wedding, ready for a fine bout of self-
pity—I'd bought a journal in which to begin "recording my
thoughts"—but Ethan disavowed it.

"Dude, *come*," he told me. There would be filmmakers there
looking for scriptwriters to work with, or crew opportunities
as a PA, working the boom mic on a shoot for a beauty school
ad or something like it.

"Stay for a bit," he said. "If it sucks, you bolt."

The party wasn't great, but it also failed to suck, which put
Ethan and me in a kitchen at 1:00 A.M., Ethan stoned to gig-
gles, listening to a woman wonder aloud to herself, "How can
someone be a magician without an *audience*?"

"Yeah, I dunno," I said, sensing the conversation winding
down, dreading the question I'd been asked four times that
evening already, bored and half-cranky about the answer I'd
given, which was the same answer I'd given for half a year.

"So that's me!" the girl said, and put her hands out. *Ta-dah.*
"What do you do?"

What I'd already told people: "a freelancer," "between jobs,"
"nothing."

What I told the woman: "Oh. I get brain tumors."

She cocked her head.

"Yeah," I said. "I walk into Brooklyn emergency rooms with super crazy brain tumors that explode in my head."

Then I put my hands out. *Ta-dah.*

Ethan revved at a low, steady snicker. The woman smiled and shifted, then looked to him as if to ask, *Is he fucking with me?*

"Tell her about Dr. Sunshine," Ethan said.

"Who's Dr. Sunshine?" the woman asked.

And with that, we were off. The circle of people that formed in that kitchen over the course of the next few minutes wasn't big—two, maybe three guys in plaid button-downs, swigging at half-warm Red Stripes—but I was now in the center of it, like I was at McKiernan's wedding, doing, apparently, what I did now. Only this was more than a constipation story: I told it all, from rupture to hospital release. The woman's face swung from concern to disbelief right at the moments I wanted her to be concerned or disbelieving. She laughed when she should have, and the guys with Red Stripes did, too. In a way I felt at home for the first time in months. Even Loren popped in from the living room to talk about fainting in the trauma ward. Given how we'd ended our trip to Ohio, I was surprised to find her next to me, so alive and eager to speak: her knees prone, channeling the viscera and flawed math of that moment through the brash charm of her own embarrassment. "I just came in," she said, "and no one even bothered to clean Mike off. Face just—blood. All over it. I stood there. Couldn't catch my breath. Then I heard the nurse say, 'Get some water. She's gonna go.' Not even a lift in her voice. 'Get some water. She's gonna go,' like people just faint all the time—which I guess if it's standard practice to bring people into recovery rooms and say, 'Hey, here's this person you love, caked *completely in blood,*' makes *total fucking sense.* Then my knees buckled"—she swayed right then left, lovely and inelegant—"and Mike's dad's right there, trying to hold me up by my arm, but I. Was. *Out.*"

Later that night, one of the button-down, Red Stripe guys walked past me as I waited to use the bathroom.

"Shit for brains!" he said, and clinked his beer with mine.

I remember thinking something that, had I said it out loud, might have sounded like *yessssssss.*

Then just like that, I got a job. It was a bad job: a four-month temp gig at a vast educational nonprofit that made a test high school students took to get into college. Each morning of my first week I walked through modest picket lines at the building's entrance at Columbus Circle, organized groups protesting the unfairness of the tests, some actually dressed as oversized pencils and sheets of lined paper, yelling, unironically, "Hey hey, ho ho, standardized testing has got to go." The nonprofit organization published volumes of study guides that they sold to high school students so they could prepare for the tests—which students also paid to take—and it was my job to secure permissions to use over two hundred different works of fiction, poetry, and journalism in those study guides.

In short, I wrote letters. I found the rights-holders to famous poems and stories and photographs and paintings then sent them

form letter after form letter, phone call after phone call, asking
if we could use their art in a book, or how much we could pay
them to do so. Then I ran those requests by my boss, Lucille, an
attorney three years my senior. Lucille's days oscillated between
uncomfortable spats of office-level zaniness and speaking to no
one, a thick air of sadness surrounding her. When I told her that
William Least Heat-Moon had sent a hand-written A-OK (in
pencil!) for us to publish an excerpt from *Blue Highways*, she
yelled, "We locked down Least Heat-Moon!" then high-fived
me and danced in the middle of the office floor. She emailed
me tips about where in the building catered conferences were
held, and I'd sneak in and steal the room-temperature pasta salad
for lunch. But other days she refused to look at me, slapping
away at her keyboard, saying nothing as I stood in the doorway
like a punished child, wondering what I'd done.

The remainder of the employees at the educational organization regarded me, a temp, as a faceless thing in a polo shirt.
I had only Lucille to talk to, and since talking to Lucille was
confusing and weird, I retreated to a kind of social paralysis,
never sure of which Lucille would show up each day and how
I should respond in return. About three weeks in, on a rainy
Friday, around lunchtime, she pushed past my cubicle wearing head gauze and an eye patch, then swung her office door
closed. It took her three hours to finally open it back up. When
she did, she called me into her office to say that weeks back
she'd been diagnosed with a rare, tumorlike ocular growth.
She'd been enduring tests and procedures like the one she'd
had today, and there were more on the way, so she might be in

the office much less in the coming weeks. I offered my concern—*oh no, sounds horrible*—but Lucille, like me, wanted none of it. She waved her hand in front of her, said that she was less scared about the illness itself than she was annoyed by her doctors' vagueness—the frustrating landscape of maybe they'd placed before her—and felt, in the throes of it, terribly alone.

So guess what I told her.

From then on we shared notes about our doctor visits, or how our medications tasted—consensus: "chalky"—and our small frustrations about the banalities of sickliness: insurance woes, the harsh, shaming tone of medical admin staff. But mostly we operated on a platform of lame in-jokes, all of them illness-based, most of them eye-roll inducing. She'd ask for a spreadsheet of the permission status for each work in our six-book volume of study guides, color-coded by who'd already given permission, which permissions required payment, and contact histories for the works we still needed permissions for, and I'd put my fingers slowly to my temples.

"Lucille, stop, *stop*—my head's about to explode."

(Again, I beat that line to a slow, slow death.)

Or she'd come to my cubicle to see me midway though leaving a fourth or fifth voicemail for the unresponsive admin person at a writer's estate, wait until I hung up frustrated, then say, "Scalise. Hey. Don't go apoplectic on me."

Or I'd take a direction from her—Lucille's eye gauze now swapped out, post-op, for a more standard, pirate-like patch that she wore under her eyeglasses—and I'd shout, "Aye, aye, Captain!" then we'd both bend our fingers into hooks.

"Arrrr!" she'd say.

"Arrrr!" I'd say back.

No one in the surrounding cubicles thought any of this was funny.

Lucille and I laughed like jackals.

Much of my time at the educational organization, though, was spent applying for other jobs. I knew I had a finite time at the gig, and while I had insurance coverage through my family's firm, it was restricted in many ways, and I was still unclear what the next steps were—what kind of procedures I'd need to remove the residual tumor, and if my Pittsburgh-based carrier would cover those procedures, whatever they'd be. I was also now tethered to my family's company in ways I'd never intended. The trick to getting me on the plan, I discovered, was to falsely list me as an employee on the payroll, and as thankful as I was for the safety net, I itched badly, beyond reasons of insurance fraud, to end that arrangement at once. I spent afternoons at the fax machine at work, sending out cover letters and CVs to every position that made sense. I trolled the internal listings at the educational organization for positions in Research & Development, Publicity, Test Proctoring, etc., and applied to so many and checked up on those applications so often that the Human Resources manager summoned me to her office on a midweek afternoon to demand that I stop immediately. The anxiety I couldn't seem to muster about the physical reality of my sickness, what did/did not happen in my bloodstream—it all seemed like a game then; I saw myself as nothing more than an automobile in need of a few simple repairs—was overruled by a creeping fear of the kind of debt I might owe my uncles and grandfather for the care of that sickness.

During my last months of college I visited my grandparents' house often, a large, white-pillared home on the fringe of a private golf course not far from the college apartment I shared with the engineering prodigies. I enjoyed talking with my grandfather about politics, if only as a means of reassurance that I was not, would never be, anything like the guy. Even so, there were parts of him I appreciated. A short man with a globe-like gut and sausage-fingers, my grandfather had a low, infectious, Santa-like laugh. He called me "Mee-szhoo Mike" and "Mike Poopacarcheck" for reasons he never explained, and seemed, like few others in my family, to be interested in things I said. But he was, like so many other Pittsburgh lifers, bitter and frightened of anyone different than him. He distrusted black people, Jewish people, Asians, Arabs. To his credit my grandfather seemed self-aware about it, looking always in our talks for ways to change those parts of himself, even if he had no intention to follow through. "Tell me what to think about these goddamned *blacks*," he'd say, the two of us sitting at his kitchen table, him nipping on a midday Glenlivet, me on whatever soppressata and sharp provolone my grandmother had left in the fridge. And I thought he meant it, that he *really wanted to know*, so in that context, disheartening as it always was, it wasn't hard to trick myself into feeling like I was doing my part in some progressive dialogue, *educating someone*, the wet dream of the young liberal.

On one of those afternoons I found him in his office in the basement, a lightless room with a wide oak desk and a boxy beige PC from the mid-nineties. It was December 2001, weeks before my graduation. Two Sundays before, I'd asked him for fifty dollars. I was readying to move to New York and had stopped freelancing. I'd quit my other jobs, and was tired of asking my parents for money. My grandfather had given it to me with little fuss. "Sure," he said, and slid a folded fifty across the kitchen table. It was the first time I'd ever asked him for money, and after years of hearing my mother's backhanded bickers about my grandfather and how he "operated," I remember being shocked at how simple it was, and how needlessly nervous I'd been to even bring it up.

"Go ahead, take a seat," my grandfather said two weeks later.

I sat in one of the two chairs positioned across from him. It was lower than the desktop. He'd been retired going on fifteen years now but still had neat piles of very official-looking papers on his desk, stacked across its surface at different heights. They looked from my vantage point like model buildings. The desk, from this angle, looked big, and the tiny man behind it did now, too. He slid open a file drawer behind him. I couldn't see it, but I heard it: the low rumble of its roll. Then with both hands he placed a thick, orange hanging folder on the open oak between us. The tab on the folder listed my parents' first names.

What happened next appears in my mind as only a montage, and I don't remember talking throughout it, or at least saying anything intelligent. But for the next hour my grandfather itemized every piece of paper in that file. It held the records of every one of my parents' assets in which he had any actionable stake. There were car leases, loans, home mortgage documents, any big-ticket payments disbursed for any reason dating back to my birth. Even the oldest documents were crisp and unfrayed. My grandfather annotated each piece of paper with a story, none of which I'd heard before: nearly every major amenity I'd grown up with—all on his dime.

My grandfather held up a pink, paper-clipped cluster of signed documents from when my father, then in his mid-twenties, ambitious but ill-equipped, went looking for a house with a nice yard for his forthcoming first son (me). Below it, another packet of papers (again, pink, paper-clipped) from when my mother, pregnant with my brother years later, wanted a house with space for two kids. This was just months after my father had tried, and failed, to run a small air-conditioning firm of his own, one for which my grandfather provided not just the start-up funds (white stapled papers, thick stack), but office rental space in the building annex of the family business my father was trying so hard to leave behind (ledger, handwritten, notebook paper).

I couldn't understand why my grandfather was showing this all to me.

"I tell them, every time, 'Why go to a bank for a loan when I can give you an interest rate half that.' Do you see what I'm trying to tell you here?" he said. "My rates will always, always be better."

I expected him to laugh that Santa laugh. He didn't. Instead he said something, many things, about "keeping it in the family." I couldn't stop looking at that pile of documents, thinking about the stories attached to them. It was, in every way, my life in bill form, or at least the upper scaffolding of it, the paperwork of my benefactors, the lives that led to my life, right there, in those numbers and staples and paper clips, sitting before me on an oak desk in a basement office. And he had the same fat files for my aunt and uncles, too, all of their lives printed up and stored in a drawer.

"Now: you've asked me for money," he said. "Not a lot, and you know I'm happy to give it—" he said, and I realized then where this was going. "I know you're going to be looking for work in New York," he said. "Going through me is better than trusting the market, especially now, so we could put you on a plan," he said, then took a paper and created what looked like a ledger. And I thanked him—"'preciate this, Pap"—even as I felt preyed upon and minuscule. I left his house determined to take nothing, accept nothing. If I was to be beholden, I told Loren later, I wanted it to be to forces I had no blood ties to.

In the hospital six months later, the inside of my head rotten with pain and loose blood, I was now on my grandfather's company's insurance plan, which I felt grateful for at the time. But now that it was over, I also wondered, in a way that kept me uneasy, *How might I be made one day to repay him for all that?*

A month into my temp gig—a little over five weeks after I'd gotten out of the hospital—I scored an interview for an editorial assistantship at a small environmental publisher. I managed to convince the hiring manager on the phone that

I was worth speaking to face to face, and for reasons too convoluted to mention, she agreed to meet me for a 5:00 P.M. interview in Central Park, just two blocks from the educational organization where I worked. It was September now. Sunlight still lingered through the early evening. We conducted the interview on a bench across the gravel pathway from a wide-trunked oak with long branches that touched down on the lawn like prayer-extended arms. Beneath them slept a tattered man and his dog, a mangy German shepherd who stood eager at his feet.

The hiring manager was a short, pleasant woman with a red flowered skirt. Any goodwill I'd built up on the phone interview was extinguished within minutes. The week between when we scheduled the interview and when it happened was, it turned out, the perfect amount of time I needed to create a doomed context for the job: the great lifeline. I'd lectured Loren nightly on its healing potential—how this job, and only this one, would lead to further jobs with bigger publishing houses, how it would give me a "behind-the-curtain look" at the industry that would help me later, as a writer, and so on. But more than that, I'd become ruled by aggressive daydreams about how this job would break me from my insurance arrangement with my family's business and allow me to navigate my illness on my own terms. I practiced answers to questions I'd been asked before, begged Loren to think of new ones to "stump" me, none of which the hiring manager asked me there on that bench, wind blowing just hard enough fold up the corners of the résumé copies I'd handed her.

We'd started out well, with a handshake and a nice, friendly talk about my history in publishing (none) and my experience publicizing things (some). Then, during an answer about my "plans for a few years down the road," I responded with, "I just want a job, *any* job," thinking, terribly, that gushing honesty in this context was a virtue. Her face turned cold, deciding—I knew this look well, I'd *majored* in getting this look—that the position wasn't for me.

My hands, already clammy, began a low tremor, my feet the same.

"I'm adaptable," I said, "and if I can just get an *in* somewhere—" I continued, and the hiring manager retracted to a steady, placating menu of *hmm*s and *okay*s. The tattered man's German shepherd abandoned his station beneath the oak tree and wandered to the edge of the gravel pathway across from us, tongue flapped out to the side of his mouth.

Our eyes moved to the German shepherd, then back to one another.

"I'll explain the process from here on out," she said, assuming a practiced professionalism. "We'll speak with the rest of the candidates—"

"Wait," I said. "Can I just show you my portfolio?"

"Sure," she said, so I handed it over: bound articles about local Pittsburgh bands, album reviews, profiles of owners of Italian delis located two whole states from where we sat. This wasn't a writing-intensive job. Nor was it a journalism-intensive one. Still, she flipped through the portfolio. It was a nice binder, built of sturdy material with a button flap, and the hiring manager skimmed page after page of my three- and four-hundred word puff pieces, the sun retreating fast behind the skyline, bitter evening wind replacing it. The German shepherd and his out-flapped tongue began, at this point, a slow casing of our miserable conversation, moving around but not toward us—behind our bench, then to its side, almost a jaunt—before returning to his spot on the far edge of the walkway.

"Very good, very nice," said the hiring manager, then handed me the portfolio. I knew it was over, another opportunity, the only opportunity. I knew we were moments from the hiring manager standing up, walking away. So I went with the only strategy that *had* worked in the last six months to make anyone interested in me, about anything.

"Can we talk quickly, before we wrap up, about your health care plan?" I said. I was a symphony of nerves now, hands on my kneecaps to halt their tremble. "I didn't know how to best say this earlier, but it's a *huge, huge* concern for me. I was just diagnosed with a brain tumor?" I said. "In my head?"

Then I pointed to my head.

The hiring manager said she was "so sorry" (though she didn't want to), and she offered her concern (which was fake), and I sputtered out the whole heaping torment, *shit-for-brains* and all.

Catastrophe anecdotes, it was clear now, had their proper context, and this was not one. The hiring manager's glazed expression became an annoyed one, her eyes desperate for escape. The German shepherd must have picked up on this. Why else would he finally move in on us in earnest, walk so softly to that poor hiring manager—right as I was about to discuss, in detail, my bullshit insurance arrangement—and place his fat head so sweetly in her lap?

"Excuse me, Mike, I'm sorry but excuse me," she said, and we turned our attention to the dog. She didn't want to pet it, but he wouldn't move, his eyes staring up at her like dogs' eyes do. She began stroking his head, fingertip swipes only, as if she was scanning his skull for braille. I stopped talking, looked across the pathway to the dog's owner, who still lay beneath the oak branches, passed out, legs crossed. Then I was petting that damn dog too, rubbing behind his sooty ears with hands I could now barely feel.

We convinced the German shepherd to take a step back, grant the hiring manager some room. It was just enough space, she must have thought, to finally bring the interview to an overdue end. She stood up sternly, extended a quick hand, and it was then that the German shepherd launched up fast on his hinds and slapped his front paws upon her shoulders, as if to slow dance. And for a moment it looked that way in Central Park, the hiring manager staggering back a few steps, laughing as she shoved the dog politely off. Then she retreated down the paved pathway—German shepherd joyfully trailing—yelling back to me, "Good-bye, good luck," as she disappeared through an underpass, taking the great lifeline with her.

CH. 7

BOX-O'-MAN

Then my father started sending me pornography. It arrived via email: PowerPoint slideshow versions of adult magazine layouts, digital flip-books that told nude, explicit, and ridiculous stories. A shirtless man in a dirty jeep approaches a sudsy roadside car wash stocked with wet young women holding sponges, with huge, silicone breasts and half-buttoned daisy dukes. Slide by slide they peel away one another's clothing and twist inside and around one another so that by the end, everyone is engorged in everyone else, sprawled all over the hood of the jeep, suds everywhere, drop-jawed and groaning.

The subject line for every email was the same five letters: TGIPF

They stood for THANK GOD IT'S PORN FRIDAY, and each slideshow had a lewd theme, some tag line that gave a preview of

the inappropriateness to come: SUMMER IN BRAZIL, MOMMIES'
NIGHT OUT, YO-YO SMUGGLERS, THONG RULES, DA CABOOSE, and
in the case of the car wash slideshow, EARLY BIRD SPECIAL. The
emails came from my father's work account, and appeared in
my inbox at the same time each week, reliable as a Sunday
paper. I kept them in a folder labeled "Dad."

He sent them, I suspected, in response to something that
had happened in the Upper Manhattan brain trauma wing five
weeks before. It was near the end of my stay. Dr. Parsens had
arrived at my hospital room, poked her head in, and asked,
"How we doing?" The spinal fluid that leaked from my nose
was on the retreat, and I was well into my flight arrangements
for Mark McKiernan's wedding the following week. Parsens
was alone now, no entourage. She greeted Loren and my parents with a tiny wave—they'd all fallen into an arm's-length
familiarity by now, an intimacy on par with that of apartment
complex neighbors—then Parsens sat nervously on my bed
next to me as if she were being held at gunpoint to tuck me
in. We'd already discussed the vastness of my hormonal fallout,
how I'd need to replace my thyroid supply each morning with
little blue pills of levothyroxine (125 mcg), and take cortisol
supplements (10 mg) twice daily.

We hadn't yet talked about my testosterone, which had,
she said, been decimated with the rest of my endocrine stash.
My pituitary could no longer send forth luteinizing hormone
to the places that that needed it (the Leydig cells, the adrenal
glands), which meant my body no longer got the green light
to produce and fuel my bloodstream with testosterone. Just like

with the thyroid and cortisol, there was no telling what my levels had been before my rupture. Parsens said normal testosterone counts for twenty-four-year-olds were between 300 and 1000 nanograms per deciliter.

My count was fourteen.

"What does that mean?" I asked.

"We should speak alone about it," she said, turning to Loren. "Is this your wife?"

"We live together, yes," said Loren.

"Well, are you—have there been any sexual issues?"

At which point my parents got up and left the room.

"No," I said. "Should there be?"

Two months later, there was email porn. But it was the second time my father had done something like this. The first time was four years before my rupture when, after I'd failed out of school in Ohio then enrolled in a community college in Pittsburgh—just an hour south of Loren's tiny school in an Amish enclave of Northwestern PA—Loren went abroad to study government in France for a year. I acted supportive but, once she left, became racked with self-pity, convinced Loren would leave me for a Frenchman with a slick beard and skinny jeans. After two years away from Pittsburgh, I'd allowed myself to regress. I drank with high school friends in their parents' basements. I fell into black moods. I stopped going to classes, and instead wrote a big, shitty novel about a college dropout who planned to infiltrate a reality television show and then off himself during a live broadcast (I'd been reading a lot of

Douglas Coupland and Brett Easton Ellis at the time). In that novel there was, of course, a twenty-year-old, non-suicidal character named "Matt," whose girlfriend, "Laura," left him to study in "Spain." I started working again as a lifeguard, this time at a hotel in downtown Pittsburgh. The only person I spoke to there was a rotund, middle-aged massage therapist who lived with his mother. He sat next to me in the warm, motionless air of the hotel pool. He'd go weeks without a single appointment, growing so bored with his own uselessness that to "keep his skills sharp," he demanded I allow him, during shifts, to knead my feet with his fat, callused thumbs.

I spent more and more time at my parents' house, sleeping in the same droopy waterbed I'd slept in during high school, eating dinner with them each night like I had as a teen. The only thing that had changed in the house since I'd left was my mother's preoccupations. She had a friend who'd started making and selling hand soap, and in response my mother launched into the latest of what was a running string of appropriated dreams, attempts to break from the family business by co-opting the ideas of those closest to her. In middle school, family friends moved to New Mexico and it quickly became my mother's goal to move there, too. When we didn't, she settled for decorating the house with paintings of mesas at sundown, cheap dream catchers and peace pipes, all still on the walls when I returned from Ohio. There'd been, sparked by the minor success of either a high school or a work friend, the great beer-making push of the mid-nineties, throughout which our countertops served as a lab station of fermenting buckets and siphons, the closets home to empty, resealable beer bottles by the case. And now, in 1998, less than a year before her first heart procedure, the dining room table was overrun with thick, wide blocks of forest-green soap bricks, the floor lined with empty gallon jugs of grain alcohol, which my mother mixed with lye to make the soap. My parents' house was as it always had been: a den of sputtered reinvention, dissolved inspiration.

Hamstrung by her late father, my mother knew little about college or what it meant (when I came home with an F one semester, she'd tried, despite my protests, to contact my professor in Ohio to request "a parent-teacher conference"). And my father had, like me, failed out. His two semesters of college were in Erie, PA, not far from Loren's current school, and unlike me he never returned, swallowed from there forward by heating and cooling, ductwork and British Thermal Units.

Which made it easy, when I returned from Ohio, to cloak my school difficulties in a sly veneer of *you guys just don't understand*. I stood in the TV room one evening that fall with my parents, pleading my case to drop out of college entirely. My mother clicked away at the computer, my father on the couch, punching the buttons of the TV remote. I stood in the center of the room, bouncing a tiny, torn Nerf basketball off the wall, reciting an argument I'd built up in my sad brain, talking about how university life was "a waste of time." In truth I'd felt failure moving in on me, fast, and wanted badly to stay a step ahead of it. But I couched my argument in the next truest reason: access to the future. I'd fallen so far behind, I told them, and Loren was actually on the other end of the earth, working for the French government, accelerating. I needed to keep up with her, with everyone, I said. College had become for me this "useless weight," I said, a heavy anchor I'd need to break from to move in the direction I needed to.

"Look," I told them. "I already know what I want to do. Why not just go do it?"

"It" was a writing career, which I couldn't have been further from. And I had no sense of what I'd need to do to move closer to that career or anything that resembled it. But my parents didn't know that, so I laid out my "plan," which relied, largely, on selling the terrible novel I'd now nearly finished, then living, I imagined decently, off of the vast opportunities it would no doubt afford. (The novel was, at that time, nearly two hundred pages long. Each chapter was written in a different font. Its title was *Twentynothings*. The chapter headings were all, no joke, lyrics from Rage Against the Machine songs.)

My mother stopped what she was doing, lit a smoke.

"If you're not happy, then you're not happy," she said.

I'd imagined her response before we talked. It went nothing like this.

"Maybe I'm not a 'college person,'" I told her, still nervous, expecting a withering retort, or at least disappointment. But my mother was warm, sympathetic. She nodded her head. She asked me what my bad novel was about ("media saturation and generational identity"), about what research I'd done for how or where it might be published (none). She talked about how, when I was younger, she'd spent quite a bit of effort researching and drafting a proposal to franchise a local hot dog and burger drive-in (the owner, who'd inherited the business, was her high school buddy). She said how much happier she thought she'd be flipping patties and serving shakes than she was running the payroll and IT departments for the family's firm. I told her how happy I'd be not having to go to computer programming and psychology pre-reqs, to just focus on what it meant to "work as a writer."

This is what people talk about when they are not sick.

"I think you should *go for it*, Mikey. Just. *Go for it*," my mother told me in a calm, encouraging tone. She seemed happy, nodding her head as if we'd broken new, helpful ground. It felt good to have an ally, to hear that I was not as wrongheaded as I secretly thought. Encouragement for a bad idea is still encouragement.

My father, who'd stayed mostly silent, listened to his wife and son discuss bold life plans beyond what he'd worked to give them, rejecting that work in no subtle way. He crushed a cigarette in the ashtray, hissed smoke from his nose.

"I can't listen to this," he said.

"What else am I going to do?" I said to him. "There is nothing *for* me in school. I'll finish the semester, then go do what I'm good at."

He pointed his finger at me.

"You—have—to finish—school," he said.

"No, I really *don't*," I said.

"I'm done," he said, then put his hands up. "*Done*. You need do some goddamn soul-searching," which is what he often told my mother at the apex of their arguments—*Do some soul-searching*—then he left and slammed the door behind him, then slammed the refrigerator door in the kitchen, then slammed the kitchen cabinet doors, then finally slammed his bedroom door.

But my mother and I kept on like we had been, me bouncing that Nerf ball again and again off the wall, her clicking away at a mouse, playing desktop solitaire, both of us talking for hours, trading variations on our own phantom futures.

A few weeks later, when I arrived at my apartment, I found a *Playboy* in the mailbox, addressed to me, though I'd never ordered a subscription and couldn't afford one even if I'd wanted to. I showed it to my roommates like I'd found a hundred-dollar bill on the street.

Playboy was in so many ways the window dressing of my adolescent home life. Below the basement stairs in my parents' house was an archive of my father's *Playboys* jammed in stacks of cardboard boxes that spanned decades. They were labeled in thick, black marker and organized by month and year, beginning in the late sixties, when my father was in high school, through the mid-eighties.

When I was an early teen and a far different kind of a hormonal mess than I am now, I accessed that library accordingly. The pages were faded and sometimes brittle. The women wore fine negligées and seemed mature and cultured and therefore irresistible, posed in warm, dim rooms with fireplaces and leather furniture. It was easy to imagine myself, even at thirteen, wooing them with conversation. But the issues were packed so tightly—my father was a ruthless collector, not just of nudie magazines but also James Bond DVDs and memorabilia, redeemable Marlboro miles, flannel shirts he wore in the seventies, novelty Zippo lighters—that it was impossible to stuff the *Playboys* back in their boxes, or even close the lids. There was no way he couldn't know that I'd been looking at them.

But he never said anything to me about any of it. My father is a thick man with a silver goatee and hard cheekbones that, despite his whiteness, cause him to resemble an amalgam of robust, bearded black celebrities. In high school my friends and I compared him to power forward Karl Malone, Steelers fullback Franco Harris, and at his most overweight moments, James Avery (who played Will Smith's Uncle Phil on *The Fresh Prince of Bel Air*). And me: I was high-strung and moody, a rail-thin stick figure who wanted to be an "artist," who won awards in grade school for my elegant cursive writing and got my ass kicked on the regular. It's not unlikely my father had resigned himself to the possibility that his son might not be interested in the idea of naked women at all. So I can only imagine his relief when I began pilfering his porn archive. *Hey: at least we agree on this.*

But now, with my two hundred pages of multi-font and my Rage Against the Machine lyrics, I saw the free *Playboy* in my mailbox differently than I had while growing up. The issue had a semiscandalous photo spread of Charlize Theron taken early in her career (traipsing around a desert landscape, waving a big white sheet). But I found I was just as excited about the short story that followed, a Joyce Carol Oates number where someone (of course) brutally murdered someone else. For days after, I told my roommates again and again with pleasant shock that "*Playboy* is actually a *really good magazine*."

The next month, after another issue arrived, I visited my parents to wash my clothes and raid their refrigerator. My father sat reclined on the couch as always, watching the film *The Presidio*, one of his favorites because of the scene in which Sean Connery, an army lieutenant colonel, beats the shit out of a bar full of drunks using only his thumb. (Throughout my youth my father had practiced that same attack. He liked to use it on me when I wouldn't get out of bed to go to school or mow the lawn or shovel the driveway or take out the garbage.)

It was the first we'd seen each other since the college-dropout discussion, since the slamming of doors, and I'd spent that time doing as he asked: soul-searching. The search wasn't long, and the verdict I came to was helped in no small way by Loren's response to my college abandonment plan, which she gave from a pay phone at a hostel just outside Normandy: "Hey, yeah, you should *not* do that."

Within a day I'd told my mother that I'd be staying in school, to tell my father that I'd "make it work." Of the ways I'd tried to force myself into a life led in opposition to theirs, I never considered that my father wanted that, too. Of course he did. He knew better than my mother that to leave school was not a corridor toward anything but the type of failure that might allow nearby forces to swoop in.

In short: My father did not want me as a coworker.

But we didn't talk about any of that that day, or any day after. Instead, when my father saw me, he said, "Hey! Shithead!" and when it was clear that we wouldn't tumble into another argument, that I was on no shit lists, I grabbed a large mason jar and filled it with iced tea like I did every day after high school, and sat next to him on the couch.

He thumbed me in the ribs.

"Want to hear something weird?" I asked.

"Always."

"I've been getting free issues of *Playboy*," I said, and I aimed to tell him that last month's issue was Charlize Theron, and that this month's centerfold featured a female professional wrestler in an almost classy spread that wasn't nearly as unsettling as I'd assumed it might be. But before I could he clapped his hands and let out a cackle.

"Ah! Your subscription kicked in!" he said. "Nice!"

It took a minute.

"Wait," I said. "Did you order it for me?"

"Yessir."

"What prompted that?"

He looked embarrassed now.

"Well," he said, then made a gesture with his hand, like he was presenting me something, "I just figured you're a little lonely, with your honey over in France. . . ."

Testosterone is literally the sculptor of men. Depending on our chromosomes, it acts as a shaping agent before birth, going to work between our fetal legs to help form the equipment that allows men to check the little "M" box under "Sex" on medical record sheets at doctors' offices, which I became quite good at following my tumor's rupture. But of the medications I took in those days, testosterone was the least masculine, at least in how I took it then. Dr. Walla prescribed me AndroGel, an odd-smelling chemical gelatin that I'd smear on my shoulder or on my belly every day after showering.

In recent years, AndroGel's profile has changed and become more prevalent, with long TV ads featuring rejuvenated, middle-aged men in pullovers and flannels—people who look strikingly like my father—slick attempts at branding ("low T"), and hushed, rapid-fire narration of the side effects (worsening of enlarged prostate; possible risk of prostate cancer; lower sperm count; swelling of ankles, feet or body; enlarged or painful breasts; problems breathing during sleep; blood clots in the legs). It's distributed now using a conspicuous, dick-looking pump, but in the early 2000s it came only in tiny foil packets that linked to one another like strands of condoms. They were often impossible to open and sometimes required scissors, and if your fingers were anything but bone-dry, forget it. I kept my testosterone packets in my medicine cabinet, next to Loren's shea butter and daily moisturizers.

Unlike my other medications, AndroGel was considered a "controlled substance" in New York. Dr. Walla had to authorize an official, notarized script for each renewal, which I then hand-delivered to my pharmacy. I reveled in the subtle power of its novelty, in imagining what the pharmacist might be thinking as I—slouched, young-faced and pasty, in my prime years for my life's highest-ever levels of T—reported to pick up what Loren liked to call my "box-o'-man." It was always off to the side behind the counter, away from the wall of traditionally filled prescriptions filed in their alphabetized drawers, alone on its own shelf in a nicely sealed brown paper bag. Each time I picked up a refill, I'd watch pleased as the tech sifted through all the typical meds in the "S" drawer, finding nothing. Depending on my mood, I'd allow it to go on for a minute, maybe two, then point and say with a calm condescension, loud enough for everyone to hear: "It's AndroGel. Right over there." Then I'd walk proud past the line at the counter, a gauntlet of the aging and busted, the typically sick, carrying my specially approved bag of dude cream.

No T had some shockingly pleasant real-world advantages. A side effect of AndroGel was that it sterilized me, sperm-wise, which fell right in line with the *no kids, just us* mantra Loren and I still clung to. We'd only lived together for eight months at this point, but had already encountered heaps of questions about our intentions for marriage and kids. Before, we'd taken a prickish, contrarian pride in the defiance—Q: "So when will we be at *your* wedding?" A: "Well you won't, because nobody will"—but now we had the far more appealing option to conspire and obfuscate. Both Drs. Parsens and Walla had said, often, that if we ever wanted to have kids we easily could, that there was a worthwhile hormone replacement therapy I could endure—a male-geared version of what "Octomom" Nadya Suleman later underwent in 2009 to have her infamous litter— but Loren and I never mentioned that part to anyone.

Instead we tucked my sterility inside a Trojan horse of trage-
dy, then wheeled it into any interaction we saw fit, particularly
the ones that happened at bars or parties, or at weddings like
Mark McKiernan's, when people who, lacking anything better
to say, asked us things like:

"So how about you guys? Kids?"

Loren would halt the moment, grimace.

"Since Mike's brain thing, it's not . . . really . . . possible?"

"My god, I'm so sorry," they'd say, then look to me, and I'd
smile, as if they'd asked me, with deep concern, if Thursday
followed Wednesday.

"Yep!" I'd say. "Brewing decaf."

My doctor-ordered stress test took place in a narrow room in
a building of the Upper Manhattan hospital that looked almost like a lab station in a high school biology room: sinks,
test tubes, Formica. It was just me, Dr. Walla's assistant Errol,
and an elevated treadmill. I was to walk on it, then jog on it,
then run on it as the angle on the treadmill gradually inclined,
as the conveyor speed increased, for as long as my legs could
bear, so that we would know my body's limits and how much
GH overflow had shaped them. Errol pressed electrodes to my
temples and chest and arms, then started in on the same kind
of questionnaire that Dr. Walla had during my first visit a few
weeks before.

"OK, so how's your vision?"

"Great."

"Do you have trouble going to the bathroom?"

"Only when I think about it too much."

He began to write that down.

"That was a joke," I said. "I pee just fine."

He asked about headaches and sleep patterns, things he'd learned from his mentor, but he stuttered and clammed up when it came to matters of my libido.

"How are things with—you have a wife?" he asked.

"I live with my girlfriend."

"Things are okay there, then?"

And I knew what he was asking, but I also knew why he skirted the issue. The majority of patients he'd seen to that point had probably hit the median for acromegaly diagnoses, middle-aged folks, and though very few of them had lost the use of their pituitaries, they were still AndroGel's target market. Whatever wane occurred in their bedroom hunger presented itself in a steady, natural arc. So for Errol—a kind man in his thirties, who'd likely experienced his own testosterone-fueled prime—to ask a twenty-four-year-old patient about his inability to have sex wasn't so much a question about the loss of a hormone than it was about the loss of a rite of passage.

But Loren and I actually had sex *more* in the wake of my tumor's rupture. As with any disaster, it drew us closer than we'd been in months, perhaps years. Yes, there was no longer a hovering danger of pregnancy, but we were also so grateful, not just for the fact of us, for our being, but for the instant trivializing of the aggravation in the months leading up to the rupture. We wanted to devour each other whole. We lost whole afternoons and evenings to one another. We canceled plans, missed lunches. Slow R&B songs played over the stereo. It was amazing and reassuring, a fervor of physicality we hadn't experienced since our very first months together as teens, during those fresh days where our hormones sent us clutching and grabbing and sniffing at one another, seizing upon reasons to knock our hungry bodies together.

But I didn't say any of this to Errol at my stress test. I was wary of overstatement, careful, in his presence, to keep things as direct and forthright as possible. "Things are as fine as they ever were down there," I told him, and even then Errol shot me back the kind of look I'd often given to people during their most desperate moments of heartbreaking transparency. *If I was that young*, he seemed to say, *it would be hard for me to come to grips with too*, and it was at that point I was sure that Errol wanted to hug me. The truth, even when I spoke it, made me feel like a fraud.

I lasted for twelve minutes on that treadmill. At the end of it, as the conveyor finally ceased, I was red and wheezing. Errol was elated, beaming. "Very, very good!" he told me more than once, then clutched his hand on my shoulder, like TV-commercial versions of proud fathers do.

That Friday, like every Friday, there was another email from my actual father, subject line TGIPF: BALD IS GOOOOOD! Contained in the attachment were thirty-eight PowerPoint slides of women with well-shaven vaginas. The women and their vaginas were in an array of locales—on bedspreads, on rope swings, in barn stables. As I clicked through them all I wondered about

logistics: who this actually worked for, who in real life mastur-
bated to those things (thanks to my wealth of early access—
aside from the *Playboys*, my father also had a small library of
VHS tapes that he stored on the top shelf of our kitchen pantry,
behind a box of dehydrated mashed potatoes: classic '70s- and
'80s-era titles like *Between the Sheets, The Devil in Miss Jones*,
and the animated, far tamer *Heavy Metal*—my tastes in pornography were, by twenty-four, far more advanced). And did my
father assemble these slideshows himself? If so, when? At work?
At home, my mother asleep upstairs? Or did he pull from some
deep, online archive of adult-themed documents, all Microsoft
Office compatible? And if that was the case, how did he find
them? What were his search terms? (When I asked him these
questions, he'd only say, "I'm resourceful.")

But mostly, as bare crotches floated in pixels past my sightline, I tried to imagine the thinking behind it, what was passing
through my father's mind the moment he hit send, pushing
over the transom to his testosterone-less son chunks of fractal
porn, one of the few things that ever truly bonded us in the
first place. *I just figured your equipment wasn't working, so maybe
these emails will help.*

"You get that email I sent?" he asked when we talked that
Sunday.

"I did indeed. Thank you for that, sir."

"I was feeling patriotic," he said.

"Bald eagles," he said.

CH. 8

POSSE

The earliest published memoir of life as an acromegalic is 1912's *Acromegaly: A Personal Experience*, written by Dr. Leonard Mark, who in his seventies set out to pinpoint the origins of his own pituitary tumor—not just when it formed, but when his growth hormone secretions began to contort him. Structured almost like a medically verified captain's log (Mark became a doctor, in part, to understand what had happened to him), the book works as a detective story of self, with Mark recalling memories or trips he took and the headaches or body abnormalities that accompanied them—"lethargy," "faceache," "noises in the head." It's a staggered, anecdotal investigation into the trail of the disease. "For fifteen to twenty years," he writes, "each day when I looked into the glass to brush my hair or shave, there was a typical acromegalic literally staring me in the face. Yet I never recognized that fact." And though Mark states up front that it's "well known how fallacious the accounts given by a patient of his own symptoms may be," it doesn't stop him from digging through and excerpting personal diaries dating back to his teens—ragelessly, regretlessly, as though he's profiling a stranger—assembling charts of his skull shape, speculating about when in his life the tumor first appeared.

By Dr. Mark's estimations, it was at age twenty-four.

My own journal as a twenty-four-year-old acromegalic was tiny and spiral-bound. I carried it in my backpack, to work, on the subway, and to lunch after my tumor's rupture, cracking it open to a clean page, pen in hand, failing to produce a single word. In those first two months, the only thing I wrote wasn't even writing at all. It was a sketch: a replica of Kurt Vonnegut's drawing of a beaver from the early pages of *Breakfast of Champions*: a crude, bucktoothed, possum-looking thing that, in the absence of more substantive material, I thought might be fun to draw. I could think of no words to describe how or what I felt then because there wasn't much to describe. When someone asked me, *What's that like each day, with the fake hormones?* I said the same thing every time—*It feels like being a left foot stuck in a right-footed shoe*—because that sounded to me like what having synthetic hormones pump through your blood should have felt like. But the truth—and what I was almost too ashamed to tell anyone then, particularly those whom I bombarded with my disaster anecdotes—was that it felt like nothing. Absolutely nothing.

Which, of course, was entirely the point. The goal was to return my wayward endocrine system to a full, healthy baseline, to make me just like every other person who walked New York City's sidewalks, who drove on Pittsburgh's parkways. At full dosage my perceptions, metabolism, and reflexes chugged at the same rate and strength as everyone else's, as they had before The Sweats and sleep apnea appeared two years before. And while yes, there were those unfit hours after I left the hospital—that guttered episode at Mark McKiernan's wedding—I often felt like I was sick in name only.

But what had happened to me (the rupture), and what was happening still (the cleaning of its mess), wasn't standard or ignorable, and in the short months since my operation there grew in me an unexpected impatience, almost a longing. I'd been impaled with needles and gauged on treadmills, sliced up and stuffed with leg fat, told by astute and impressively degreed professionals that I lacked ingredients essential to my lifeblood, and part of me yearned to feel as torn-through as I was told I was now. I wanted to sense the extent of the damage, the trace of its shape.

I often thought of the nights, after her first heart procedures, when my mother would sequester herself on the back porch of my family's house in Pittsburgh, wine-soaked, piling kinked butts into ashtrays as my father, brother, and I moved across the first floor of the house like a shark's remora, glancing through the window as we passed by, moving around my mother but never toward her, wary of being pulled into her low atmosphere. I thought of the nights during my last months in college, when the phone would ring in my apartment, usually well past ten o'clock. A quiet hold of seconds before a version of my mother's voice emerged, then tumbled into the beats and themes of her last phone call and the one before that: loose, aching hems and haws about whatever artery renovations were on tap in the coming weeks or months. "I don't think I can do it again," she'd tell me. "I must be like your damned grandmother," she'd say, "not meant for this world." The calls would last hours and go nowhere. Sometimes I'd snap back—"You gotta quit *talking like that*"—but more often I stayed silent on the line as she rolled around in the same phrases, the same guilt, the same defeat, exasperating us both. "Okay, Mom. Okay," I'd say. "Please. Get some sleep." I was so overcome by resentment after those calls, turned livid by the way my mother seemed so easily to give over to what I saw as a bullshit failure narrative.

But in this fresh era of hormonelessness I began, in a very faint way, to envy my mother's sullen intimacy with her body's breakdowns, her ability to snatch them up and lock them in her brain, commune with them even, her constant, resigned retreads building into their own brand of anti-mantra. For all the bravado I showed in public, the shit jokes, the wit of character—and it truly felt like that, a role I inhabited—in my private moments I couldn't lock on to a single thread of insight or introspection about anything.

On a weekday, at a bookstore a few blocks from my house, and with no counseling from experienced people whatsoever, I bought a how-to book on meditation: the first one I saw that seemed simple and graspable, with a title like *The Novice's*

Guide to Inner Balance. The next night, with Loren gone for a shift at Angry Wade's, I folded my legs in a lotus-cross on the warped hardwood of our apartment and attempted, as the manual instructed, to "shut my mind off" and breathe, to "disconnect my brain from my body," and so on.

But I was far too self-conscious, even home, even alone. There was no shutting-off or unplugging from one prevailing thought—*what the fuck am I doing right now*—and though I tried again, and again, I abandoned each session, nagged by the worry that I was, after all that had happened, a poseur, a loudmouthed paper champ of my own rare illness.

Then there was the matter of my appearance, which my doctors told me had changed, which articles that friends and aunts and cousins sent me said had distorted my temples, brow, and jawline, plumped my hands, hardened my skin. But as with Dr. Leonard Mark, I saw none of it. Not as it was happening, not when Dr. Parsens and her team measured changes right in front of my eyes, and certainly not now, two months later, when my mother—taking a welcome break from the kind of conversations I'd been used to having with her—became excited about the realm of pituitary abnormality, at least as much as her cable package permitted. When she called now it was well before ten, and the voice on the line was quick and fascinated, playfully urgent, alive in the world of my illness in a way I couldn't seem to be.

"Quick, quick," she'd say. "Your tumor's on TV."

I turned on my television. On the Discovery Channel or TLC or a channel just like it was a pseudo-documentary, an exposé on medical hiccups rare and unexplained, featuring a midthirties woman living in Memphis—small, blonde and angled, fat hands, brow hovering over her eyes like an awning—who'd gone months without her period. Fearing she might be pregnant, she'd visited her primary care therapist, then after that an OB-GYN, who'd referred her to an endocrine doctor, who took a look at her temples and forearms, asked how she was sleeping (terribly, of course), then scheduled the girl for a tumor removal in two months' time.

This gave the producers of the program the opportunity to take a break from the girl's own burgeoning narrative as an acromegalic to explain the long history of the disease, a Ken Burns–type photo swirl of oblong heads and bent bodies from many decades or centuries past, sepia-toned forms twisted into something resembling punctuation—all men, all of them barrel-chested, facial contours bulbous and exaggerated; wide, fleshy mitts and gnarled back curves.

My mother and I watched quietly together, the audio on her TV in Pittsburgh an echo through the receiver as the program flashed forward to a more recent montage of the featured young woman's own shape: modern, full color this time, Dorothy in Oz. There were medical mug shots, both face-forward and profiled, the woman stripped pale to her bra and saggy underwear, graphic lines appearing onscreen to highlight her concavities, the shifts in her posture.

And then, soon enough, the operating room shot, surgeons ringed around the woman's split-open face—for her entryway, they removed the stem of skin between her nostrils—and yep, there it was, round, red and smooth: my tumor on TV.

In the years since my diagnosis I've become a human way station of pituitary factoids, a cataloger of stories about growth hormone and brain tumors, attuned to the mainstreaming of acromegalics, how they're floated into the public consciousness. The show I watched that night with my mother in 2002 profiled a traditional acromegalic, but most of the shows I've watched on the edutainment channels of the basic cable era (I have seen so many of them), and most of the online information about pituitary tumors (I have viewed so much of it) provide, at some point, a bridge to the more well-known, more fantastical cousin of acromegaly, *gigantism*.

In many ways it's the exact same condition, just with an earlier birthday. For gigantics the tumor occurs when the body's bone cartilage is still open to hormonal interpretation—often during puberty—allowing the GH overflow to go quickly to work, expanding far more than just the hands and feet, but the arms, legs, chest, back, shoulders and head as well, turning a real boy or girl into a walking mythological figure.

But in terms of pop culture shorthand, the two conditions are almost interchangeable, lumped into the same phylum of pitied, dehumanized monstrosity. Take, for instance, the opening scene of the 1955 film *Tarantula!*, in which a barren desert landscape is populated only by a hump-shouldered man walking stiffly to the center of the frame, his massive forehead shiny above his skeletal brow. A violin swells. The figure snarls and writhes beneath the sun, moving with terribly wooden, zombie-like struts toward the camera before he collapses to die, his oversized, veiny hands clutching the loose sand.

The man, we soon learn, is one of several "nutrient biologists" in a small-town Arizona lab who's injected himself and a number of test animals—one of them a tarantula—with the experimental "nutrient type 3Y," a strength serum whose side effect is a rapid-form version of what's referred to in the film as "acromegalia" (ack-row-muh-GAY-lee-uh). People are injected, turn acromegalic, ransack or set fire to things, then die. There's a detective on the case, an investigation into experiments, and a lab mishap that results in the injected spider escaping, expanding, then terrorizing the town, growing larger, skyscraper-sized, swallowing herds of cattle whole, depositing ponds of what one character calls "insect venom in the large, economy size" next to its victims. The acromegalic spider keeps doing this, unstoppable in its hunger, until the townsfolk rally, then summon a crew of fighter planes to napalm the thing to a fiery death.

Roll credits.

Then there's the plot of 1944's *The Monster Maker*, which follows the story of a mad scientist who—convinced that a famous concert pianist's daughter is somehow the ghost of his dead wife—finds a way to poison the pianist with a serum labeled ACROMEGALY B-5 B-7. In just forty-eight hours the serum renders the pianist's head ghastly, his hands too plump and deformed to tinkle the keys. "Not only are his fingers incapacitated for the intricacies of delicate performance," says the mad scientist, "but his very appearance, upon which so many depend on for public approval, is most uninviting." But it's re-vealed, of course, that the mad scientist has been in the acro-megaly-dosing game for quite some time, starting with his dear departed wife, whom he tracked down and injected after she left him for another man. Within days she committed suicide because, as the doctor puts it, she "could not stand the sight of her own face."

It was through this realm of freaks and monsters that many real-life acromegalics entered into showbiz. In the 1940s—an era that birthed films very similar to *The Monster Maker* and *Ta-rantula!*—a man named Rondo Hatton carved out a fine niche for himself as a mainstay of cut-rate, Ed Wood–type horror pic-tures like *The Spider Woman Strikes Back* and *Johnny Doesn't Live Here Anymore*. Hatton was, like me, an acromegalic minus the gigantism. He was my height, six foot one, and his WWI expo-sure to German mustard gas likely triggered his tumor growth, leading the man, after a short career as a journalist, to be the go-to ghoul of the B-flick set. Voted "Most Handsome" of his high school graduating class, GH overflow turned him into what one paper called "the kind of guy who could give a girl nightmares," a body twisted into striking, unexpected angles: linebacker shoulders and a brick-shaped chest, a long face of deep valleys and wide curves that inhaled the backlit exposure used in the films for which he became known. He played his most famous character, The Creeper, in both sequels to *The Pearl of Death*, a role that elevated him to such cult status as a villain that, well after his death in 1946, his autograph remained a sought-after collector's item. (Hatton's likeness has since been recreated as a twelve-inch, fully pose-able action figure with "crusher" hands and, for whatever reason, two interchangeable hats.)

Hatton was followed in the 1960s by Eddie Carmel, another fringe actor who was named "world's tallest man" by Guinness and, like Hatton, parlayed it into minuscule roles in mad scientist–type flicks like *The Brain That Wouldn't Die*. Carmel was an acromegalic giant, with a crooked, scarecrow frame billed at eight foot nine (though some put him at just over seven feet), with a childlike, jar-shaped head, jug-handle ears, and a sweet/sad-seeming demeanor.

In his twenties, Carmel attempted a career as "the world's tallest comedian." During that time he produced two 45s, "The Happy Giant" and "The Good Monster," that, unlike "Monster Mash"—the single they're clearly modeled after—failed to chart well. Carmel finally caught a break at thirty-four as the focal point of a photograph by Diane Arbus. She titled the portrait "A Jewish Giant at Home with His Parents in the Bronx, N.Y., 1970" and it ran in *Time, Newsweek, Life*, then landed at the Museum of Modern Art, where it now sits on display. The photo shows Carmel in his parents' living room, hunched over them like a tilted human question mark. His mother and father stand next to him, shrunken ellipses, staring up at their son like he's broken something. "Why did it have to happen to me?" Carmel later said about the photo. "My luck, I have to have midget parents."

There have been others since. Lurch from the '90s' version of *The Addams Family* (real name: Carel Struycken). Jaws from

the Roger Moore Bond films (Richard Kiel). NBA center
Gheorghe Muresan. Herman Munster (Fred Gwynne). God-
father of the infomercial and "Authority on Peak Performance"
Tony Robbins, whom I'd watched often on those apnea-
riddled nights leading up to my rupture, and—in a bit of news
that made the rounds shortly after my diagnosis—Olympic
champion figure skater Scott Hamilton.

What this means is that when you're diagnosed with acromegaly—when you arrive home from your typical doctor visit
about your sleep problems, sit down, and type that word into
the Google search bar, hoping to find out who you are now,
what context you're now tethered to—you learn at once that
you've been placed on a very particular spectrum of ugly. You
learn you're a human sample of an oddity, part of a small family
of conditions so obscure and strange and disconnected from the
mainstream illness zeitgeist that people frequently don't consider the fact that they actually exist as real ailments (see also:
leprosy, Ambras syndrome, progeria), despite the fact that an
estimated 20 percent of the world's human population harbors
your same tumor, undiagnosed. You learn that your condition
is one that gives over to hour-long basic cable documentaries
about the real-life examples of what you'd thought only existed in a Grimms' fairy tale, a Coney Island sideshow.

And if you're like I was, you have no idea what to think
about any of it. I was angry, yes, but it was a nebulous anger,
and directed at whom? At the examples, for existing? At myself,
for not noticing earlier? For still—even with all the knowledge
of what the tumor had done to my body—being unable to

truly see it? The people around me, for not being more force-ful months earlier? Would anything have been different if they had? I still felt spellbound by the phantom limb of my own self-image, how I'd always thought I'd looked. My doctors *told* me my brow was distended, my temples were caved in, my hands were big, and my tongue was fat, but in my mind's eye they weren't the day before that, or the month before that, or the year before that. I'd just looked like *me*: long face, shark-fin nose, slouched posture. The influence of self-image is a deep one, and it certainly doesn't yield objectivity, so what else is there to do, post-diagnosis, but tuck away that aimless frustration and con-tinue believing I was still living in the image I'd always known?

And nothing I saw—not on the Internet, not on pamphlets, not on basic cable—was any help. The pseudo-documentary that I watched that evening with my mother in 2002 *appeared* more generous and sensitive toward the depictions of acro-megalics past than what came before—the human-interest arc, the sad history of pituitary hideousness—but it was, I knew even then, an illusion of audience. That show wasn't for me. It was *about* me, explaining me to non-sick people, or at least the me I'd been told I was now, the me I couldn't seem to see. I wanted, needed, the opposite.

"Don't you feel lucky they caught it when they did?" my mother asked before we hung up the phone that evening.

"Oh yes, absolutely," I said to her, wondering what, exactly, luck was supposed to feel like.

Within that rogues' gallery, there was no acromegalic giant more famous, more known, or more referenced than André René Roussimoff, a.k.a. Géant Ferré, a.k.a. Monster Eiffel Tower, a.k.a. Andre the Giant.

Mount Rushmore–like in his prominence as a studio wrestler through my youth, Roussimoff had left his home in the French Alps at fourteen, already over six feet tall, then moved to Paris, where he was discovered by promoters and put on an international wrestling circuit. At seven foot four, over five hundred pounds, he rose quickly through the ranks of the 1970s' burgeoning studio wrestling culture to become the sport's most decorated champion and largest draw until 1987, when he was famously body-slammed in front of a crowd of thousands wrestling his biggest rival, Hulk Hogan (a.k.a. Terry Bollea), who then went on to eclipse him.

But only in perception, in broadcast theatrics. Roussimoff was someone who, unlike any other wrestler or acromegalic, lived as large as his myth. He was diagnosed (like me, at twenty-four) with a pituitary tumor while wrestling in Japan. He decided against surgery, choosing instead to take what the condition gave him and answered it with what can only be described as lifelong, complicated bluster. He liked to talk Archimedes while drinking nearly two hundred beers in one sitting, or reminisce about his rides to school as boy, when he was chauffeured by, and talked literature with, his neighbor Samuel Beckett. He took prank shits in hotel bathtubs. He starred in Rob Reiner's classic *The Princess Bride* as (what else) a giant who liked to rhyme.

In the fall of 2002, Andre also lived large in the minds of lower Manhattan primary care physicians, at least when I visited them. On top of the stress tests and the bone density readings (so far, so good), Dr. Walla had given me one last, important assignment: to find a lazy doctor. She needed full control over shifts she'd need to make in my medications, she told me, complete rein over any tests she'd need to order. She couldn't be troubled by a primary care physician who was a stickler about referrals and, given my precarious insurance coverage, thought the best move was to find a primary care physician who would be amenable to what she called a "nontraditional arrangement."

In other words, someone who simply didn't care. In the two weeks since my first meeting with Walla, I'd already ruled out three. Their waiting rooms made them uniformly promising as candidates: itinerant, bitchy desk staff, unkempt chairs and floors, a crowd of fidgeting patients waiting angrily for repair, walking to the sign-in post at the receptionists' desk only to be ostentatiously ignored. But the doctors themselves were either too young, too eager, or both, their eyes wide when they read the words ACROMEGALY and HYPOPITUITARY on my clinical sheet. I distrusted the origin of that excitement, the weird hunger they displayed, excited to have even the mildest version of a freak show on their patient roster.

"Oh, I've *read* about this!" they'd say.

And: "*This* should be interesting."

And there'd been a point in each of the first three exams when they'd stop me midway through an explanation of my insurance arrangement, my need to turn everything over to my very important specialist/hormone detective and say, as though I hadn't already known, as if every single person I knew then hadn't already told me, as if this bit of trivia wasn't the instant freebie chunk of pop culture given to everyone upon their diagnosis of a pituitary tumor:

"You know who had acromegaly, don't you?"

"I do," I'd say. "Andre the Giant."

My diagnosis came just over a decade into a guerrilla street art campaign headed by provocateur Shepard Fairey (later of the ubiquitous Obama/HOPE poster of 2008), who in the early nineties made a name for himself by launching a propaganda-like graffiti experiment he called OBEY: posters and stickers slathered across cityscapes that featured extreme close-ups of André René Roussimoff's face. Only it wasn't Roussimoff's *actual* face. It was a facsimile of it, morphed into a slick, stark Rorschach mesh of black and white. From one angle the posters showed the wide, expressionless face of the lumbering wrestler from my youth; from another, a blooming mushroom cloud that stemmed from the bridge of Andre's formidable nose into his expansive forehead. By the time my tumor erupted, Fairey's experiment had snowballed into a worldwide phenomenon of Andre-faced branding. It was, ten years after Andre's death in 1992, almost as commonplace as the real André Roussimoff had been for decades in his heyday. Fairey's work was placed around New York like a brooding, second skin. After my diagnosis, I saw it everywhere: plastered in mosaic on construction enclosures, slapped in sticker form on the stems of street lamps as I walked from my apartment to the subway, stenciled on the sidewalks in the Upper Manhattan neighborhood blocks surrounding Dr. Walla's office, and, most notably, on the lower Manhattan city blocks of the primary care physicians I was now in a position to audition.

Those auditions would end the moment they mentioned Roussimoff. I'd hear that name and move right along to the next doctor on the list. I wanted examples of acromegalics who *weren't* novelties, I would tell myself as I boarded the train back to work. Then my eyes would fall onto a sidewalk stencil or a streetlight decal featuring (who else) Andre the Giant, the patron saint of acromegaly. He was peppered along my city pathways in images I'd never cared about before, images that now claimed my eye, like random photos of lost loves and mortal enemies stuck to the side of buses. The wide nose and mouth, the droopy bell curves of his fist-like brow—features that I had, apparently, now inherited to a degree I couldn't determine— came into my sightline whether I wanted them to or not. OBEY, the images often read, or just as often, and with irony I was all too aware of, ANDRE THE GIANT HAS A POSSE.

By late October I'd settled in well at the educational organization. Lucille and I had grown closer, no doubt due to our paired catastrophes. Lucille promised me work for as long as I'd need time to find something more fitting, careerwise (read: *not* permissions for study guides), and we talked often about the state of our illnesses. She'd been cleared of all possible malignancy for her own tumor, the eye patch long gone. She was patient and understanding as I missed work to perform Walla's tests, or to hoof around the streets of lower Manhattan and Brooklyn to find a lackluster PCP that took Pennsylvania insurance.

"Oh, go to my guy," she said. "He doesn't give a shit."

Her guy's office was downtown, on a nice block with a large, empty waiting room, and the doctor himself was staunch and bearded, hovering around fifty. He looked me in the eye only to say "Hello" and "Goodbye." His office was vast, and we were there ten minutes, throughout which he stared at my clinical sheet, then the floor, and little in between.

"Famous disease," he said. "Abe Lincoln had it."

"Is that true?" I asked.

"Maybe. I think I saw it on a website once," he said. "He was tall. I know that."

And with that I hired the man, then I never saw him again.

CH. 9

ANOTHER ONE

During high school swim practice one afternoon, a girl I'd hoped to have sex with announced that she'd formed a theory on how to build the perfect man from three members of the team. Using, I assumed, some human amalgamation contraption, she said she'd combine the face of freestyler Patrick Kormos (square-jawed) with the body of breaststroker Jake Abrams (wide-shouldered, muscular); then finally, into that new, attractive Frankenstein, she'd pour a personality.

Guess whose.

Her plan struck me, though, as surprisingly fair. I'd sensed somewhere around sixteen—when my bump-middled "Roman" nose suddenly overtook my face's real estate—that I was slated to be a power-of-personality type. Before then I'd wondered about my appearance, but not much; just a creeping, back-of-the-mind suspicion that I was maybe not the best-looking guy in the world. When the verdict finally came, there at swim practice, I was pleasantly unhurt. The news was soothing, helpful. I knew at last where I stood, which freed me to hone that personality, an effort that eventually yielded Loren, someone so objectively stunning that my friends—and sometimes just random people—often asked me: "How did *you two* happen?"

"She lost a bet," I'd say, especially to other women, who would later confess to me in a curious tone that I enjoyed for many reasons, "Loren is *beautiful*." I took it as a subtle confirmation that I understood how to package myself in a way that counteracted my middling features.

And let's be frank: tumor or no, my body had been straying from baseline for years. I graduated high school a gaunt six foot one, 140 pounds, and while that version of me was essentially how I still saw myself, by age twenty-four I was easily 70 pounds past that. The word that comes to mind is "galoompy." Loren, though, didn't seem to mind. "When you were skinny I used to like skinny guys," she once told me, shortly after I moved to New York. "Now, I like them a little fuller."

As with any weight gain, it never seemed irreversible. And if there was ugliness it was homegrown: *my* ugliness. I understood its origin (nose, eyes = Dad; facial shape, body = Mom). However unimpressive, I knew my own image, liked it, owned it, and assumed I'd one day muster a return to its best version, the version so tattooed in my mind that it stopped me from seeing anything else.

Days after I watched the pseudo-documentary with my mother, on a cold Saturday afternoon, Loren bought albums to organize the photos she'd kept in the wooden crates that doubled as our bedside dressers. We spread them out on our living room's hardwood floor, piles of photos organized by era, then spent the late afternoon filing them into slots. I uncovered a photo from the infancy of our relationship, taken shortly before we left for college. In the photo we're dampened, seated in some low-end restaurant booth. Loren looks refined, even at eighteen. Her dark hair's strands are wet and long, her white neck is exposed. My face, on the other hand, is a downturned guitar pick. Tan and long, unripe but smooth, skin draped over my cheekbones in a seamless curve, disappearing to a point at my prim jawline.

I took that photo directly into the next room, then snatched another pic that Loren had taken of me no less than a month before my rupture, one she'd said I "look cute in." I'm standing on the wooden walkway of the Brooklyn Bridge, far off but alone in the center of the frame, hands at my sides, sweating (of course) through a yellow, collared golf shirt—a hand-me-down that belonged to my father when he was twenty-four. Based on everything Drs. Walla and Parsens told me later, this was around the tumor's fifteen-month birthday, and the body that hosts it in that photo is heavy with a deep tiredness. A backpack hangs from my slackened shoulders. My head now: blocklike, the angles of my cheekbones and temples jutted, almost octagonal, hard and lopsided against the down-pouring sun.

I held the old photo alongside the new one, my eyes switching between them, matching up the silhouettes, interpreting the outlines, trying to determine which force had more influence on me over the six-year span between: time, or the tumor.

"You can see it here, right?" I asked Loren, holding up the Brooklyn Bridge photo.

"See what?"

"In the temples and the jaw," I said. "That's clear, right?"

"I like that picture," she said. "You look nice."

"I *know* you do," I snapped. "But can you please look?"

I handed her the new and the old, and she glanced at them, put them down.

"We're *children* here," she said, pointing to the high school pic. "Children look different than adults, baby."

That night Loren and I brushed our teeth for bed, huddled around our tiny sink, bobbing into it like oilfield pumps. I caught my own image in the mirror, just stayed with it. No photos. I rubbed my fingers along my temple's contours, felt the turns of my cheekbones, and tried to disconnect myself from my mind's best image.

"Ok, yeah, you can see it, right there," I said. I grabbed Loren's arm. "Look," I said. "You can *see* it, right?"

Loren rested her toothbrush on the sink, then put her lips to my temple's edge, leaving toothpaste froth on the concavity I could neither measure nor look away from.

We sat in a spare Chinese restaurant on the Lower East Side—me, Loren, Ethan, and his Jersey-born girlfriend, Juliet—picking at a basket of steamed dumplings, boring Juliet to irritation with another round of Pittsburgh talk, minor updates and opinions about non-New-York-living people that existed in our collective memory bank. Juliet was young, blonde, and quick. An assistant to the assistant of an insanely well-known morning talk show host, she possessed charmingly little ability to hide her displeasure regarding time of hers that we'd wasted.

Ethan was retelling the same story he had two weeks before, about a mutual, old friend from high school who, while overseas teaching European businesspeople how to speak conversational English, had been deported for mysterious reasons from the country where he'd lived and worked. As Ethan once again unspooled his theory as to why—Juliet interrupting, "We know, hookers and knives, you *already told them this*,"—I decided for the sake of newer material to move the discussion, firmly, to the realm of ultrasound jelly.

Earlier that day I'd been lost in the nether regions of Queens, shuffling through traffic gaps beneath subway overpasses in search of the lab Dr. Walla had set me up with for my ultrasound test. I arrived nearly forty minutes late, worrying that I'd missed my opportunity and might need to reschedule, but the place was nearly empty, save for a small, kind ultrasound tech who smiled when she saw me, said, "Let's see how you're doing," then squeezed a pile of clear gelatin into her hand.

At dinner that night I told Loren, Ethan, and Juliet what it smelled like (sweetly pleasant, like hair product), how it felt when it was rubbed on my chest (cold, weird) then combed over by live transducers, and what it was like to watch a spotty, glugging feed of my heart chambers on a computer monitor (surreal, intimate, a little gross).

But Juliet, of course, had been hearing me talk about this kind of thing since July. She'd heard every iteration of my brain tumor stories—she and Ethan were, in many ways, my test audience—and this she time stopped me midsentence and said, "You know, my mother had that same tumor."

"*A* brain tumor or *my* brain tumor?"

"Same as yours," she said.

"Nuh-*uh*."

"Yep. Same thing."

"How old was she when they found it?" I asked.

"She was thirty. She was in the hospital after giving birth to me."

"How did she find out?"

"She was knitting, in a hospital bed, and she went to bite a piece of thread, to break it off, and she noticed her teeth didn't line up. Her jaw was distended. So she asked her doctor about it."

"So her tumor didn't rupture?"

Juliet shook her head no.

"Wow," I said. "So what does *she* look like?"

"Like my mom," Juliet said.

That weekend I stopped by Ethan and Juliet's apartment to meet Ethan for a movie. There she was, Juliet's mother, reclined

on the futon, the only acromegalic I'd knowingly met in real
life and, years later, the only one I've knowingly met since. I'd
never been on a playdate, but the energy in that apartment—
Ethan at his computer, stitching together his reel for a freelance
gig, Juliet pointing to me as I walked through the doorway—
felt, I imagined, like it might for two toddlers arranged into a
fast, faulty friendship.

"Hi," I said.

Juliet's mother moved at me with a swift gait—clearly she'd
heard there was *another one* out there—and I studied her as she
did. I was tall, but she was diminutive and wide, a tan, squat
woman with a bowlegged waddle and a compact brutishness.
Juliet never mentioned how long the tumor had worked undetected on her mother's pituitary—and frankly, it didn't seem
wise to ask—but it looked to me, as her features got closer, like
decades. I took in Juliet's mother's face, as I imagine she did
mine. Hers was frog-like. I remember this clearly. Her thick lips
seemed to stretch the width of her jawline, her brow hanging
over her blue eyes on both sides like the foot of a bell curve,
all of it built around the buried outline of a soft, emotive face,
which I recognized only because it lived now, undistorted, on
the head of her daughter, who stood between us.

The whole encounter took no more than a few seconds.

"Lemme see," Juliet's mom said, then grasped my head like
a hunk of produce. I felt her hands and she pushed them over
my head, down my face. They were large and lukewarm, the
skin on them tough, jerky-like. I went limp and passive. But I
wanted to. I wanted Juliet's mother to be my acromegalic elder,

my inductor, someone of authority who could at last confirm the image that had appeared to me in the bathroom mirror weeks before. It was all I saw now, the octagon of my head, the hard angles of my new face. And beyond all other desires, I wanted to be done wondering where the boundaries were, where I ended and acromegaly began. *Yes, you've been shifted,* I wanted Juliet's mom (or anyone, really) to tell me, *and here is exactly how,* if only to be able to move on, to begin to construct a way, like I had in high school, to build something more of myself than my muddled appearance. *If someone were to build the perfect acromegalic,* I wanted to ask her, *which parts of me could they use?*

But Juliet's mother held my hands up to her face, shook her head, almost disappointed, then let them fall to my sides.

"This is nothing," she said. "You have nothing."

PART THREE

CH. 10

BAIT

atastrophe anecdotes thrive on a confluence of timing, context, and conversational opportunity. But
those elements rarely align perfectly, which is why
it's helpful to have on hand a form of bait; an artifact from
your terrible event that can nudge your audience toward a
single question:

Hey, where did you get that?

At work, my bait was a boxing nun. It was a finger-action
hand puppet I got as a get-well gift during my stay at the
Upper Manhattan brain trauma ward. Once I settled in at
the educational organization, I brought it to the office as a
matter of "cubicle personalization." Lucille and I named her
Sugar, and she stayed mostly in my desk drawer. But sometimes she made late appearances at happy hours or holiday

parties to pelt the faces of drunken coworkers with her tiny boxing gloves.

After a few quick jabs—Sugar led with her left—I was fielding the right kind of inquiries, undoing the invisibility of my status as a temp. "Oh, I got her in the hospital," I'd say, or: "One of Loren's college friends shipped her to me while I was in recovery." But I made sure to mention it with flippant ease, at which point the conversation was all mine for the steering. And where did I steer it? Wherever I wanted, which was always away from acromegaly, away from any discussion of enlarged hands or giants, and quickly toward trivia and puns about shit-for-brains, anything to make my voice quicker and more engaging than the visuals—whatever those were now.

I planted several other pieces of bait throughout the folds of my compact life, each one a dangled carrot in the face of general discourse, waiting patiently to be asked about. The *best wishes during this turbulent time* greeting cards that hung open-faced on our fridge. The stationary set from Jean the VFT tech, which sat conspicuously on an end table.

Some worked well, some not at all. Almost three months after my operation, I still wore the hospital pajamas Loren had stolen for me from the brain trauma ward. They were white, flannel-soft, light as a bedsheet, and throughout the days I spent waiting for my brain wounds to reseal, I went on and on to Loren, my parents, and any other patient soul about how comfortable they were, how the draw-string stayed tied no matter what, how they *didn't even ride up*, and so on. I wore them nightly to bed once I got out of the hospital, all day around the apartment on the weekends, sometimes even to run neighbor-hood errands like grocery shopping or refilling medications.

Then, around late October, I walked into our bedroom to find each pair in a pile at the side of our bed, next to the radiator. Loren stood not far away, loading old clothes into bags for secondhand donations.

"Can we donate these?" she asked.

"They're my PJs."

"Can we get rid of them?"

"But they're so comfortable," I said.

"I see those things," she said, a hairline break in her voice, eyes slick with tears, "and all I can think of is that hospital, and you in that bed, and they even *smell like that place*—"

No more pajamas after that.

Most of my other bait was weeded out in a similar fashion (Sugar met her end about a year later, during a sad act of clutter-pruning when we moved to a far smaller apartment a few blocks away), but the one bit of bait Loren seemed not to mind keeping around were the x-rays. They featured before and after shots of my brain at all angles: from above, from behind, profile-like. Some were tumor-free (*after*), and some showed a thick, unruly spatter of white behind my eye sockets (*before*).

"Check this out," I'd say when people came to our apartment, then slap them flat against the sunlit window in our living room.

"It looks just like a cartoon brain looks, right?" Loren would say, and our poor guests would nod and point and say, *Wow, that's amazing*, in a deadened tone one might reserve for enduring a gauntlet of vacation slides, which, in essence, these were.

I got ahold of the x-rays after my stress test and my chest ultrasound, during my first trip back to see my neurosurgeon, Dr. Elmer, since my discharge earlier that summer. His office was a high-ceilinged, red-carpeted corner room on the first floor of the brain trauma ward, and we were there to discuss how to handle what was left of the tumor. It was hard for me to sit still. I'd become strangely unmoored about how to conduct myself now that I was not Elmer's critical task, his leak in dire need of a plug. The morning was cloudy, flashes of rain spittle. As Elmer talked I glared through the street-level windows at cigarette-puffing nurses, shifting in my seat, faking comfort in an over-starched blue oxford and khakis. My neurosurgeon looked at the scuffed backpack puddled at my feet. He asked me if I'd "just come from class," and seemed not to believe me when I told him I hadn't.

"See all this?" Dr. Elmer said. He pointed to his computer monitor, which was the size of a wall poster, at the spatter of white on the *before* slide, behind my eyeball.

"Is that it?" I asked.

"Well," he said, "it's the blood *surrounding* it."

He pointed to the *after* shot and showed me my carotid artery, which ran like a thin vine down the length of my neckline. He traced his capped pen over the area—"Here's our guy," he said—then pointed to a spot behind my eye sockets, a small nodule of white.

Or I think that's what it looked like. I couldn't tell what I was seeing, but I was hesitant to ask for more clarity. Dr. Elmer's demeanor during my operation prep had been clipped and diligent. He'd never stayed at my bedside for more time than was necessary, and instilled awe and obedience in his underlings by being brief and inaccessible. I appreciated that. It felt good to be under the care of someone with such resolute arrogance about his ability to repair all of it. His office was an extension of that resolve. Where Dr. Walla's office was unadorned and spare, almost bunker-like—just that neat little plastic cross section of a brain, nothing else—it was difficult, even as Dr. Elmer showed me my own head on a screen, not to let my eye drift, to mentally catalog the certifications and awards on the bookshelf behind his wide oak brick of a desk, the framed photos of his wife and polo-shirted sons, the binding thickness in the volumes of craniological casebooks aligned next to one another on the lower shelf like pillars. For the first time since my rupture, I felt like I hadn't deserved the quality of care I was receiving, that I should just feel lucky to have this portion of Dr. Elmer's busy time, and to ask for anything would expose me as a freeloading interloper.

So although I didn't see the residual tumor he was pointing to, I acted like I did. I nodded my head, said, "Yep, right there," then crossed my arms as he moved on to talk about regrowth, which he said was "something we'll need to stay ahead of."

There were two ways to do that, he told me: one a diet of self-administered shots of questionable efficacy that aimed to make small, daily dents in the residual tumor's fortitude. The second, more experimental, and possibly more effective option was the very new, very cool-sounding Gamma Knife radiotherapy treatment. For this he handed me a pamphlet with bulleted information and photos. This form of radiotherapy was far different from that of cancer patients. It was localized, with few side effects, and delivered by an MRI-like machine that looked in the brochure like a room-sized, flipped-up toilet seat with an outstretched tongue. According to the text, Gamma Knife shot "photon radiation" at "variably shaped targets ranging from several millimeters to more than three centimeters in diameter" to the slice of tumor still squatting inside my skull, looking to resurrect. The only catch, Elmer said, was that there was little data to support Gamma Knife as a fail-safe option, and that it might be years—three, maybe five—before the radiation took full effect, if it took any effect at all.

"The shots, we can do here," Dr. Elmer said, "but the Gamma Knife we'll have to coordinate with another hospital."

"Any recommendations?" I asked.

"They have a *great* machine in Pittsburgh," he said.

CH. 11

WHAT ELSE CAN SHE
GIVE BUT HER MILK?

My brother wanted to come to my second MRI. It was scheduled for December 23 at a wing of the University of Pittsburgh Medical Center just blocks away from the apartment I'd lived in the year before. He was home from his first semester of college in Indiana—like me, he'd managed to vacate Pittsburgh, at least at first—and we sat with my mother and father at their kitchen table, chewing on sandwiches of roasted red pepper and prosciutto, crumbling slats of sharp provolone. My mother had shifted her interests in recent months to the world of online stock trading—the television, for the hours I'd been home, was set to a financial news station polluted with NYSE crawls and Neil Cavuto's head—and as she talked about her recent "finds" with my father, my brother pled his case to be my MRI accomplice.

He said he felt "like shit" about "missing out" on the event of my rupture. My brother had said this often in emails, phone calls. I'd assured him throughout my stay in the brain trauma ward—and then in weeks and months after—that there would have been nothing for him to do there, that his concern was more than enough (which it was), but my brother wore his guilt heavy at dinner, whining with an annoying, convincing sweetness, "You're my *brother*. I want to *be there*, you know?" So although I'd come to covet the solitude of waiting rooms, my alone time with the contraptions that studied my guts— it was, I'd begun to realize, the closest I'd come to meditation—I felt I had no choice but to say yes, great, it'll be nice, bring a book.

It was Christmastime, yes, but it was also the six-month anniversary of my tumor's rupture. I had been ordered by Dr. Walla, my neurosurgeon, and the Gamma Knife team at the UPMC Center for Image-Guided Neurosurgery to get a follow-up scan of my brain so that Walla and my neurosurgeon could troll for signs of regrowth. The Gamma Knife team needed them to begin early calibrations for radiotherapy. It would be the last procedure before, perhaps, my last procedure.

As much as my brother was hoping to "be present" for my MRI—and it was, I'll admit, nicer than I'd realized to have him there—after a few minutes in the dark, lightless waiting room at the UPMC Radiology Department the next afternoon, my brother made it clear that he'd also been looking, desperately, for an excuse to leave the house.

We'd grown up nearly six years apart, and were only just discovering ways to be more than shit-heeled nuisances to one another. We were careful now to respect each other's coalescing identities as near men. It made our conversations oscillatory and intense, swinging from the loose, everyday—my brother liked to tell me about the parties he'd gone to with his college buddies, the same kinds of things he'd heard me talk about when I was in college—to the deeply personal and confounding, such as my mother's unpredictable disposition which, apparently, had been erratic enough to drive my brother to a midafternoon reprieve in a colorless MRI waiting room.

My last trip home had been just weeks before, for Thanksgiving, when my extended family converged on my parents' home with hugs, handshakes, and opinions. It was the first I'd seen my parents since they'd left New York in July, but it was also the first I'd seen my extended family since weeks before the rupture. Sensing they'd carry with them a certain collective curiosity, I'd brought my newest form of bait: the initial *before/after* films from my summer stay in the brain trauma ward.

But apart from a few quick *Hey, you OK?*s, my family seemed far more interested in matters of status quo. My grandfather took his seat in the corner rocking chair, and his sons spread across the couches and chairs of our living room. The women, as always, stayed in the kitchen to work on the meal. The men fell, like they always did, into rote, unsubtle cuts at one another about management decisions and on-site productivity, rumors and likelihoods regarding certain contracts up for bid in the coming months. It was an insular, boring rhythm we all knew well, so when my uncles started in on my father's middling golf game—they like to get on him about his slice—I decided to step in.

"So," I said. "Who wants to see it?"

I kicked off with the *before* images of my tumor: the fat, wide ocean of white behind my eyeballs. "It looks friggin' *huge* there, right? That's just because it's bleeding," I said. "We'll never be able to tell the actual size of the tumor. We'll *never know*—" etc. Then on to the *after* images, where I circled my finger around the tumor-less space like my neurosurgeon had weeks before, mentioning the residual tumor, its possible regrowth. "Right here, by the carotid," I said, though I still couldn't tell what I was pointing to. I talked about the groundbreaking Gamma Knife, making sure to highlight that it was home-based, right here, in town.

"Turns out the two best places in the world to have a pituitary tumor implode are New York and Pittsburgh," I told them. I knew it wasn't true—there are machines in Florida, Philadelphia, and San Diego, just to name a few—but I got to watch my grandfather smile and nod, and my uncles follow suit. By the time I was on to "brewing decaf" and ultrasound gel, my brother had cracked a beer, leaned against the near wall. My mother, aunts and grandmother had come in from the kitchen and sat at a nearby table with their full wine glasses, sinewy branches of cigarette smoke braiding in the air above.

My mother was laughing. It was a suppressed, reminiscent laugh, the kind people leak out from the safe distance of a calamity's memory. And she was laughing again many glasses of wine later, stopping me as I walked by to hug me for long, uncomfortable spells, her face buried into my chest.

"I'm so glad you're home," she said.

"Glad I'm here," I said right back.

But the next night, after I'd come home late from a night out with friends, she was alone and awake at the kitchen counter. The iced Pinot, the un-ashed cigarette.

"You scared *the shit* out of me," and so on.

Days later, after I'd returned to New York, back into the context of my illness, my father called and told me that just before the holidays—before I'd walked in with my brain-splatter microfilm and my tap dance—my mother's cardiologist had discovered, on her own semiannual inspection, another artery blockage in need of a stent. The procedure was scheduled for the coming summer. It would be her fourth.

In the UPMC waiting room for my MRI, my brother told me how my mother had, in the two days since he'd been home for Christmas, kept my father up to all hours, nervously rehashing scenarios and fears ("I don't think I can do it again") which my brother had heard clear upstairs, over the blaring TV in his old bedroom. My brother told me how she'd lit into him for not spending enough time at home, how they'd already had two screaming fights regarding the issue.

"The trick is to let her run her course, then forget about it," I told him with the false assuredness of a weathered veteran, as if I had ever done the same. My brother, prideful and short-tempered, said he'd watched for years as she and I went back and forth. He knew what he needed to do. We treaded in that slow conversational space for several more minutes in that waiting room, trading best practices for passivity, until a radiology tech—a thin, squirrelish woman—emerged from the back-room lab holding a thick folder.

"I knew we had *one* Scalise boy coming in," she said. "I don't think we have enough room in that machine for the two of you."

My brother looked puzzled.

"Howdy, Mrs. Barb Antoncic," I said, for his benefit. Barb Antoncic was a mainstay at the public pool I'd lifeguarded at through high school and parts of college, the mother of Bill Antoncic—a thin, squirrelish presence throughout my elementary and middle school bus rides—and his thin, squirrelish sister Jamey, who'd once made out with Jeff Stibner during a house party I threw in high school, then spent a grand portion afterward vomiting malt liquor foam into my mother's front bushes. This is how Pittsburgh works.

Once I robed and slippered up, Barb Antoncic asked about my parents—"Good," I told her; the answer to that question is always "Good, great"—then she smiled and said, "Watcha been up to these days?"

I clammed up, unsure of where to begin or what to leave out, but almost immediately I realized that her question was a courtesy. She was holding my medical records.

"Weird couple months," I said.

Barb patted the table of the MRI machine like it was a bunk bed. "Climb on up."

Of all the procedures I'd had, MRIs were my favorite. I'd heard damning things about the nebulous terrors of the process—the maddening tightness of the corridor, the jackhammer clang from the frequency coils as they conjured images of your insides. But that's what I loved most about them. To my senses, they were a soothing, rhythmic drone. I fell into it so easily. With my head hugged on both sides by fiberglass walls, pinned there like the neck-injured people I'd saved as I lifeguard, I felt safe under the invisible waves of that grand magnet, serene and tucked in, hidden from all intruders, asleep in minutes.

By the time the smelts hit the table on Christmas Eve, by the time the hubcap-wide dish of broccoli linguini took its place along the pizzelles and calamari, the meat and cheese, by the time my grandfather told me, again, how he'd driven my grandmother to the Copacabana for their first and only trip to New York, by the time my aunts and uncles and their children sat in a ring in my grandparents' living room to peel open that year's fleet of toys and unwearable sweaters, my mother had already fallen ass-first into the Christmas tree. It was a quick fall. Aside from my father I was the only one in the room to see it. She'd just stood up from the couch and taken a step, then at once she was upon its lowest ring of branches, among the bulbs and lights. It was as if the wide Douglas fir had yanked her toward it, her arms up, palms forward, some low, confused moan, when my father, just as quickly as she'd fallen, scooped her up like a wayward toddler. Without a word or a glance in my direction, they both walked right back into the kitchen. Not a bulb fell from a branch.

My mother was drunk, but to be fair, so were all the women who hovered at their stations around the stove. The effort was led by my grandmother, my father's mother—a cranky woman with a love for fart humor and raw, lame jokes (my favorite of her go-to's: "What did Adam say to Eve in the Garden of Eden? *Here, pull on this thing and see what comes out*")—and my uncles' wives all worked under her direction. My aunts, like my mother, were well over the porousness and pageantry of the family business hierarchy, the who-gets-what, the beholdenness. There'd been a revolving door of aunts, people who'd come into my uncles' lives—some left children behind, some didn't, some were left behind *because* they didn't—and so the aunts struggled during holidays to team up, though their ability to put away deep pours of Chardonnay seemed their only binding talent.

Like the others, my mother resented holidays at my grandparents' house, particularly after the death of her own mother. While my father's parents lived just yards from the back nine of a private golf course, my mother had grown up two miles away, in a small home on a gravel road that was kept afloat in the years after her father's death by her mother's maintenance and the lean pension left from her father's career as a railroad worker. Holidays at that house were simple, the gifts modest and useful. My mother's brother and sister had rallied around their widowed matriarch most readily during those times, helping with the casseroles and pork chops, often inviting nearby neighbors to share in meals to the point where I considered many of them uncles and cousins well into my adult years.

During downtime each Christmas at that tiny home—Stroh's bottles and cheese puffs, knitted afghans folded over the couch—my mother and her siblings filled the gap their father had left with conspicuous reinventions of the man, vignettes they seemed to regard with a reverie that confused me. "For swim lessons," my aunts and uncles would tell me as a child—my love of swimming the only thing they really knew about me—"your granddaddy would take us to the lake and make us swim. Indian-style." When I asked what that meant, they told me he'd bring each of his kids into a lake or pool then make them swat at the water like a tomahawk, their frightened bodies tightened even more than they already had, plunging fast beneath the water's surface. "He'd yank us up and laugh," they'd say, "then he'd tell us, 'Go ahead, try again.'"

All of the stories of my mother's father were like that: demeaning, trivial pranks played on his unsuspecting children. My grandmother, even more so after her stroke, turned flat and wordless when they told these stories, sat low on her rocking chair in the corner with a slow-burning Salem. "He'd tell us riddles," my mother told me often, "then leave them to us to figure out." I can recall, secondhand, only two. The first: *A car and a car and a car can't go, and that's the way you spell Chicago.* (Answer: *Shit, car. Go.*) The other riddle my mother said she never solved, one that her father went to his grave without revealing: *What kind of cow gives only buttermilk?*

(Answer, thanks to the Internet, just now: *What else can she give but her milk?*)

But after her mother died, whatever was left of my mother's bond with her siblings died as well. There were disagreements about who would handle the affairs, then arguments about the avoiding of the handling of the affairs, then even sharper disagreements about the choices made by those who finally *did* handle the affairs. The house they were raised in was rented out, and with no neutral ground on which to conjure spirits each Christmas, communication lines between my mother and her siblings weakened and in some cases severed. My mother sometimes went years without a word from her brother or her sister in New Jersey, even after her sister began having her own heart problems. As a result, Christmases became for my mother extended gatherings with her coworkers, bosses, and her father-in-law, my grandfather, the boss of my mother's bosses—the man who owned the mortgage to her home; the man who my mother told me had once, while she was dating my father, called her "trash" to her face. But with no family of her own now, my mother was expected to be present in the world she'd married into, to participate in discussions about fair clubhouse fees and try-hard debates about Montepulciano vs. Sangiovese without the reprieve of driving down the road to crack open a Stroh's.

Perhaps she was thinking about all of this when it came time to open presents on Christmas Eve in 2002, her mother gone eight years. While the smallest of my cousins passed gifts to each of us—my aunts in folding chairs next to their husbands, my round-bellied grandfather in a high-backed chair next to my grandmother, his plump fingers folded across his chest—

it's possible that my heartsick mother was thinking about the making of ghosts, or what ghosts had made of her, or—with her fourth stent procedure on deck—how those ghosts had returned to her in forms far different than she expected.

I don't know what was on her mind then. As I stood in the threshold between the kitchen and the living room, watching as my youngest cousin tore away a flap of wrapping to reveal a mint-condition, classic Barbie figure—which gave way to bickering amongst the adults about how removing the figure from its original packaging would cause its future value to plummet, how the classic Barbie should, above all, be viewed as an *investment*—all I heard was a sound. We all did.

It came from the my mother on the couch, who sat now with her back erect, hands on her kneecaps. Her face was ruined. Her eyes were closed. She was howling. I smiled at first, thought it might be a joke. But the howl blossomed into a slow, earthy wail, something high and terrible. Then she took a breath and began again. "I'm sorry. I'm so sorry," she said, almost as though she couldn't stop herself—breathing deep and wailing, her nose sprung with clear, long leaks, the room frozen around her, stalled with—what? Concern? Disbelief? I went breathless. I didn't move. My eyelids grew heavy. My ears felt plugged-in, submerged. "I'm sorry everyone," my mother said, and for a few long seconds after she said it, no one said anything back. My brother, sitting on the nearby stairs, met my eyes briefly, then looked down to the carpet and didn't look back up. A weakness sparked in my gut. It traveled through my ribs, to my fingers, feet, and chest, and I slid my newly numbing hands into my pockets, pumped them for feeling, as my father embraced my mother and she leaned into him, and my Aunt C. moved next to her on the couch and held her hand. In seconds my mother was unruined again, and we were all back to the gifts, holding up scarves and gift cards and nose hair trimmers, saying thank you, hugging each other, saying goodnight. All the way home my mother smoked out of an open window in the car, December wind sneaking through, hitting my brother and me, silent in the back seat—me still pumping my fingers into fists, like the nurses at Dr. Walla's office often asked me to do in order to coax blood flow for tests, but now I was doing it to coax back sensation, which was not working—until my father pulled us into the garage and, escorting my slushy mother like a reluctant prom date, took her, and himself, straight to bed.

What my brother and I did: smoked all the Marlboro Lights we could find. Drank all the booze in the house.

CH. 12

GAMMA KNIFE

The good-natured nursing staff at the UPMC Center for Image-Guided Neurosurgery kicked off the morning of March 18, 2003, by sitting me on a gurney, pumping me full of morphine, and encasing my head in an inverted steel halo—what they called a "stereotactic frame"—which they fastened to my skull with an electric drill. Two holes right in front of my temples, where horns might be, and two behind my ears. Then the head nurse stepped back and took aim with a Polaroid camera.

"Little souvenir of your time with us, yeah?"

I said something innocuous, like "Sounds good" or "Let's make it happen," then sat up in my hospital bed and lifted my chin. My father stood quietly along the wall beside my mother, who appeared raw and weary. I peeked out at them from behind the steel halo, which was meant to secure me to the huge machine warming up in the next room, set to feed my brain tumoricidal radioactivity.

I was excited. I'd been assured by my specialists in New York, as well as by the director of the Center for Image-Guided Neurosurgery, that the procedure had a near-airtight effectiveness rate and that the lone side effect was a bout of mild nausea, so I primed myself for it as one might for a camping trip or a bungee jumping excursion. I'd spent the previous evening with old friends brainstorming hypotheticals for happy accidents, most of which involved heroic mutations. A spider finding its way between the radiation beam and my head, perhaps. Rage-induced green skin. I took all the doctors' suggestions and brought my most comfortable pillow for the two-hour procedure, along with an excellent mix CD for them to play over the loudspeakers.

"Give us a little smile?" the head nurse asked, and my mouth loosened to a drunken, toothy grin. As the Polaroid's flash sparked the room, my thumbs shot up like a rookie pilot about to lift from a carrier.

For the half-day following my Gamma Knife treatment, my head was charged with fresh radioactivity. The amount was small enough to present no danger to anyone around me, the nursing staff insisted, yet they still reserved me a hospital room by myself until the next morning. My mother, father and I spent the afternoon eating dry, flattened hamburgers in the hospital cafeteria, reciting bad passages from a sportscaster's memoir that they'd picked up for me from the campus book-store blocks away, the place where just over a year ago I traded in overpriced poli-sci books for lunch change. We didn't talk about the episode at Christmas, or the one before it at Thanks-giving, at the sink, the "you scared the shit out of me." Like all the episodes before it, and all that would come after, they sim-ply disappeared during daytime hours. For my mother it was as if those episodes existed within their own, steady continuity, one that never bled into her sober life.

I was thankful for her amnesia. The cheeseburgers were hor-rible. After three bites I peeled off the top bun of the burger—a patch of the cheap, airless bread still clung to the patty—and said, "Look. Guys. It's my brain."

"Needs ketchup," my father said.

Within minutes my mother was laughing with my father about some indecipherable, morphine-laced nonsense I'd let loose just before the treatment. I tried to reenact it, but it wasn't as good.

After the trip we'd had to the Manhattan hospital last sum-mer, and the trips to Pittsburgh hospitals we knew were com-ing, Gamma Knife radiotherapy, for all its threatening syllables, seemed almost like practice, a move through the motions. For the remaining hours of the evening my mother, father, and I (my brother was at school, banished from disaster again), the three of us glancing cautiously to one another, each now too weathered in this kind of thing, yet still a touch too supersti-tious to say what I could sense we were all thinking: That's *it*?

PART FOUR

CH. 13

A CERTAIN KIND OF BUSY

The woman who interviewed me at the children's publisher was brisk, tan, and Australian, with a warm wit and a disarming forthrightness. I wanted to work for her immediately. And after that Central Park interview the previous fall, I understood now that the best way to be taken seriously for a job is to act like you could do without whatever they're offering. After Gamma Knife I picked up freelance gigs, and I'd gotten real cracks at positions throughout Manhattan— one for a permissions assistant at a gargantuan, midtown media compound that had flat-screen televisions built into walls of the elevators, which in the middle of 2003 was goddamn fancy—none of which offered more, benefit-wise, than what I had already. So while my mind was a steady drum of *yes* and *now* throughout my interview at the children's publisher, in that conference room I sat loose-shouldered in my black sport coat, and told that Australian woman about editorial schedules and XML coding and using content management systems as though they'd been the fabric of my work life for years, which they very much had not. But it didn't seem to matter what I could or couldn't do, only that I didn't seem worried or overly excited or nervous about any of it. I made tepid jokes, she laughed. She made tepid jokes, and I did the same thing. Weeks later, for the first time, I had my own health coverage.

And what did I do to earn that coverage? I wrote instruction manuals. The children's publisher made a reading program which they installed on computers in elementary and middle school classrooms around the world. The program was loaded with "multimedia options" and "data aggregation capabilities," and I wrote the books that told teachers what all of that meant—terminally boring, all of it. But I liked the challenge of acting as an interpreter. I'd never taught in a classroom, and had done little more, tech-wise, than attach a photo to an email. Yet each new set of instructions I wrote was an opportunity to gain a very particular kind of control over a tiny realm of unknowns—every checkbox and drop-down menu, each new development in the program's vast armada of features—until I knew it all so well and gained enough power over it to shrink its vastness, and show laymen and technophobes and grade school teachers the easiest, most direct ways to make something complex and powerful work seamlessly for them.

I liked that job, but it wasn't my favorite among the several I had. A few months after Gamma Knife, I'd begun collecting them. My salary, like many young publishing salaries, was barely enough to live on, so I took a part-time gig in a dingy penthouse at a midtown marketing firm four nights a week, pecking out trivia questions about product placement in television shows like *Trading Spaces* or *American Idol* or *Monday Night RAW* for an online game designed to fleece brand knowledge from pop culture geeks. People like me.

Here's how it worked: if, for instance, I watched the show *Cops*, and a speeding motorist drank a clearly visible can of Coke while he/she was pulled over by that episode's police force, I wrote a question like this:

What did the red-haired man in the pickup truck do when Detective Smith finally pulled him out of the car?
A. Ran into the woods
B. Dropped a bag of narcotics on the road
C. Began crying hysterically
D. Offered Detective Smith a sip of cola

If an online player—I should note that I never encountered these "players," and never met a soul who had—chose the correct answer (D), the website then auto-revealed the next question:

What brand of cola did the red-haired man offer Detective Smith a sip of?

A. Pepsi

B. Dr. Pepper

C. RC Cola

D. Coke

A correct answer here (D) set off a chain of ready-made follow-ups, plodding marketing inquiries about how that player felt about the motorist's Coke: if it was distracting, made them more or less likely to buy Coke, more or less likely to watch televised lawbreakers, and so on.

I got paid sixteen dollars an hour for that.

In my downtime, when there was any, I wrote columns and technology pieces for a glossy trend magazine, and profiled couples who built their homes around their multiple cats for a fluff quarterly aimed at "animal lovers and pet parents," which featured in each issue a spread of the latest trends in canine fashion as well as a "Letter From the Editor" written by a terrier named Lucky.

I would have written for anyone about anything. After Gamma Knife I told myself that it was over, that the needle on my life's record had reset to pre-tumor days, and resumed the same untamed, professional relentlessness I had at the end of college. It was *do something or die* all over again. There were whole weeks where Loren and I didn't see one another for more than one waking hour. I'd slide next to her slumbering body after a 2:00 A.M.–late Thursday, thanks to *Extreme Makeover: Home Edition*'s endless shots of Craftsman tools and Kenmore appliances, each of which required a specific trivia question (*What brand of free-standing range did Ty Pennington install in the Dobelcheks' new kitchen?*). Then I'd wake up at 7:00 A.M., push through a manuscript deadline, spend lunch interviewing pygmy horse trainers for a "guide animals of the city" feature to be turned in that weekend, then hope for enough time, somewhere, to fit in a four-hundred-word column about the ubiquity of gadget addicts for a seventy-five-dollar contributor's rate.

I was awash, gladly, in a certain kind of busy. Most of my daytime coworkers at the children's publisher were spurned but hopeful Teach for America vets pushing hard at better-paying educational careers; calm, resourceful women who spoke impressively and off the cuff about classroom management strategies and "think-pair-share" activities, who spent long days prepping marketing presentations they'd give nationally: PowerPoints of new software features narrated by characters from my childhood books, or songs with lyrics full of educational buzzwords, sung over copyright-approved instrumental versions of ' '90s Top 40 hits like Montel Jordan's "This Is How We Do It."

My nighttime coworkers at the trivia job were eager, snobby filmmakers, writers, actors, and journalists whose evening job kept them free during daylight hours to audition, write spec scripts, pitch stories, and assemble their reels. Everyone there was broke and anxious and insecure. But it wasn't enough just to run ourselves ragged in order to prove fit for the lives we claimed we wanted. We had to also spout long, detailed confessionals over whiskeys and sidewalk cigarettes about how viciously we were doing so.

Throughout all that talk with the trivia writers I rarely brought up my brain tumor. For the first time in nearly a year, I didn't need to. The trivia writers talked about movies and television and music and movies and books and television, the kind of pop fodder that passes for meaningful discourse among people of a certain age and inclination, the secret-twin language of the bookish and media-bathed, of which I was definitely one.

It was like the end of college, but better, more informed. Each trivia writer came with their own trail of disparate experience, half-baked achievements that had yet to fully rise, and every word they said was refracted through that small prism of authority. There was Sal the Former Stringer for the *New York Post*, Laura the Auditioning Stage Actress, Robb the Freshly Graduated NYU Lit Major, Josh and Dylan the Aspiring Sitcom Writers, Diane Who Pitched Headlines Daily to *The Onion*, Juni the Endlessly Displeased Wannabe Literary Agent, and Nick the Unassuming Standup Comedian Who Once Advanced to the Semifinals of a Reality TV Show. After Friday night shifts we'd abandon our stations en masse, commandeer some dim, inexpensive dive on the Lower East Side, then flood the place with shoulder bags and movie quotes and fiercely defended opinions (on Nabokov and Dave Chappelle, on sports and comic books, on the New Pornographers and Elliott Smith, on Charlie Kaufman and Joan Didion) until the 4:00 A.M. last call, after which we moved as a blithe, stumbling flock out onto the barren sidewalks, then fell into cabs bound for outer boroughs, only to reconvene just hours later, pissy but unfettered, to write multiple choice questions no one ever read about a four-hour-long NASCAR event none of us would ever personally watch.

It was as if we'd found, by virtue of our devotion to modern ephemera, a clear, unique home for ourselves among the entanglements of a city of eight million. It was nice to come into work in the evenings and see two people huddled over a laptop in the break room, pouring their efforts into some scriptwriting program, or to grow perturbed by the length at which the two people sitting next to me debated a recent online album review for some indie band I'd never heard of, then further, the complete body of music reviews that the online author had contributed, talking as though that writer had somehow formed a canon-in-progress, something worthy of awe.

The trivia job could be annoying in that way, but given all other alternatives, it was a good annoyance to have, and I was a little less eager in this atmosphere to step back beneath the public umbrella of my illness, to become Mike the Guy with the Sort-Of Andre the Giant Disease but Maybe Not Anymore, especially now that I had the chance to be Mike Who Can Identify Every Quote from Every Movie Released After the Date of His Birth, or Mike Who Works at a Children's Publisher and Writes about Pygmy Horses and iPod Accessories—all of which fit the identity I'd intended for myself a year before, or at least a facsimile of it.

But there were still nights when I couldn't stop old reflexes from taking over. One night (or morning?), I sat with the trivia writers at a small outdoor beer garden in Brooklyn with one-dollar hot dogs and two-dollar tallboys—we'd all had plenty of both—talking with Frank the Recent Fiction MFA Grad and his girlfriend, Audrey the Hilarious Sex Columnist, both of whom worked the home improvement reality shows with me in the evenings. Frank wore smart-looking glasses and a goatee, Audrey a buoyant white dress with orange flowers the same shade as her ponytailed hair. We argued, at more length than the topic deserved, about whether a well-known writer—whose pop culture–laden novels had been made into big, pop culture–laden movies—was or was not "a hack," as Frank put it. Frank thought so. Audrey disagreed. I rode the fence and said he wrote funny scenes, but called his subject matter—mostly relationships, or white guys' tired inability to commit to them—sophomoric and trod-upon, which probably left my mouth that night as something more along the lines of "trite bullshit."

"That's not *my* reality," I told Frank and Audrey, and soon enough I was talking about what, exactly, my reality *was*, what it had been for the last eight months, then the last two years, and how the one thing that hadn't changed, surprisingly, *was* my relationship to Loren, how our commitment to one another had thrived in its wake, had been the lone constant. Frank and Audrey looked surprised, then concerned. It occurred to me that they didn't actually know about the brain tumor, that I'd been talking to people about my tumor so quickly, so often, and for so long that I'd begun to assume it was my personality's understood preamble, that by now everyone must have already known. (I'd gotten a call not long before from a girl

I dated briefly in high school, and I started the conversation with "So you heard about the tumor, huh?" "I was calling to see how you've been," she said. "What tumor?") Frank and Audrey didn't know anything, and when I mentioned it, they had questions.

I wasn't emotional when I told them about it, but I wasn't exactly tap-dancing either. Frank asked me what happened with the rupture, and I explained it. Audrey asked what the effects were, and I listed them. It was cold but straightforward. What materialized around strangers as a need to perform became, with Frank and Audrey, a flat impulse to confide.

"And I *look* different," I said.

The server thunked a fleet of tallboys onto our table.

"How so?" Frank asked.

I was pleased, briefly, that they hadn't been able to tell already, that I had to actually explain.

"You know how Andre the Giant looks?" I said. "In the Shepard Fairey posters? Wide jaw? Caved-in temples?"

I twisted my head under the gleam of the overhead light, traced my fingertip down the slope edge of my right eye, down the curve line of my jowl, detailing a progression. Maybe. I hadn't done anything like this since the run-in with Juliet's mother months before. Since then I'd become a conversational detective, listening for telling details in the ways people referred to my physical features, to see how they matched up to the acromegalic I still maybe/possibly/probably saw in the mirror. I read deeply into any hint. Someone at Angry Wade's—where Loren was now, slogging through a shift a few blocks down the street—once mentioned that my handshake was "enveloping," and I'd stared at my right hand for weeks. Now I was laying it out for Frank and Audrey, swiveling my beer-heavy head for these kind people at 2:00 A.M. like some slow, neighing horse, hoping—as I had for months—for anything that resembled an objective verdict on what I looked like.

"I have no clue what you looked like before," Audrey said. "But I like your face. It has *definition*. You look *chiseled*, you know?"

I cracked open a tallboy. *Definition. Chiseled.* There was a comforting politeness in Audrey's words, a movement toward a compliment. Yet I distrusted them immediately, was struck with the impulse to chase after whatever I thought she was covering with courtesy, to interrogate what those words meant and how exactly they applied to the angles of my face, or maybe even explain to Frank and Audrey what *I* saw now, what I couldn't *not* see.

But instead I nodded, said, "First I've heard that one," then thought it wise to change the subject to something more easily categorized, like movies or music or television or, please, absolutely anything else.

Days later Loren and I sat in our living room, staring at an empty coffee canister and a twenty-four-pack of syringes. Dr. Walla wanted to place me on a regulatory agent, something called *Sandostatin LAR*, designed to defeat the GH-Releasing Hormone (or GHRH) still leaking from my residual tumor, which is a complicated way to say it was a hi-fi Band-Aid on my bloodstream, designed to hold it in check until, or if, the radiation took effect.

But the Sandostatin shots were so potent that my body had to first develop a tolerance. So for weeks I carried with me a package of low-dose, disposable one-offs, and a coffee can for "bio-responsible needle disposal," then plunged a shot into a "fatty portion of my body" three times a day. I took great pleasure in unearthing those syringes from my shoulder bag while at the educational publisher, then announcing loudly to the former K–12 teachers in my surrounding cubicles each day just before lunch, as they worked on group activity binders:

"Okay, folks. Time to go shoot up in the men's room."

But most of the Sandostatin warm-up shots happened before work, on our couch, while the local 24/7 news channel played its endless loop on our hand-me-down TV. Loren and I would lean against each other on our futon. I'd take out a tiny syringe—the needles were about a quarter inch long, each shot felt like less than a bee sting—and locate a fresh patch of skin to jab. Each time I'd ask Loren, "You want to do the honors?" and each time she declined. But this day, when I asked, she smiled slowly and sat up.

"Fine," she said. "Give me one of those things."

Loren maintained that eager grin when I handed her the syringe. I pulled up my shirt and held out for her a large flap of skin from my belly, which wasn't hard to do now. The subcutaneous fat deposits produced by my chalky cortisol pills (along with my near-complete lack of exercise) had, over the year I'd been taking them, turned my gut into something far more garish and distended than it had ever been; round, large, and unignorable.

She pierced it with a calm, intent joy, then sat back, coldly flipped channels, and talked about the day ahead. And I—the pale, shifted version of someone she'd overcommitted to as a child, hands larger and rougher than she ever expected to hold, whose face now was a dubbed-tape version of the one she fell in love with, *chiseled* in a way I still couldn't properly take in—stared toward the same TV, trying hard not to look at the nearby framed photo of us in that restaurant booth at eighteen, trying hard not to ask myself: who, exactly, was Loren finally so pleased to stab?

CH. 14

THE MOST LITERAL POSSIBLE
UNDERSTANDING OF THE WORLD

I think it was the tanning that finally did it. It was early June, almost at the one-year anniversary of my rupture, and I was with Dr. Walla in her office, sitting across from her, waiting for my first full-dose shot of Sandostatin LAR. The late morning sun cast a long stripe of light on the worn peach carpeting. Walla had my file spread open in front of her, two high stacks of notes and exam results. I wanted to know why I couldn't tan. She'd just finished one of her lead-off surveys (*Are you sleeping well? How's your energy?*) and I'd asked her why my skin seemed to actually *reject* sunlight now; why for a year it had been borderline translucent, sickly looking and corpse-like; why the most common remark I got from people since fine weather had reemerged in full was, without question, *Jesus, dude. Get some sun.*

I'd been trying. We'd had a sun-filled spring. I'd spent free Saturdays riding water taxis to Manhattan, then blanket-lounging with Loren in the shadeless swatches of Central Park. I'd sat for long, bright hours with Ethan and our friend Leigh on his Hell's Kitchen rooftop, playing video games on a television set we powered using two linked extension cords we dropped down to an outlet just inside Leigh's fifth-floor window. On the evenings I wrote trivia I walked from Job A to Job B, a slow stroll up Broadway to Madison Square Park, watching the sun slump fast behind the shoulders of the skyline. I was outside as much as outside would have me, and still, not one hint of a farmer's tan. Not even a slight bronze on my neck, no ring at my sleeve line or shirt collar. It used to be that I wouldn't have to try, that within hours of stepping into a beaming day I turned penny-dark. My grandfather, uncles, and Loren liked to joke that I looked "fresh off the boat," and it had been that way throughout my career as a lifeguard, throughout college, and up to the tumor's rupture. Photos from just a month before my diagnosis show someone with a big nose that's red and shiny, skin a deep olive. But now, even after weeks beneath the sun—no sunblock even—my skin managed at most a light, rosy burn, one that dissolved within a day's time.

Much later, I'd read and learn more about MSH—melanocyte-stimulating hormone—which my lifeless pituitary failed to send to the cells in my skin that required melanin for a healthy tan, rendering me forever pasty. But in Dr. Walla's office, just a year after my operation, I noticed a schism between her goals as a doctor and mine as a patient. Walla seemed concerned only with testing metrics and medications that would repair a uniquely broken body. Her training was in data and guesswork, response and re-measurement: this was how she had built her career as a researcher. Whereas I—who *lived* in that body, who reluctantly embodied all that data—sat in her office still very confused and frustrated about what was broken, and how. I wanted answers and rulings, boundaries and certainty.

When my tumor ruptured it seemed like Dr. Walla had a plan, a Phase 1, a strategic assault on the tiny slice of rebel tumor, the eradication of the acromegalic forces in my bloodstream. As a patient, I found this comforting in its thoughtlessness. *Take these pills. Get these tests. Absorb this radiation.* Phase 2 struck me as too theoretical and unguaranteed. I had a terribly unseasoned ear for my own body, which I'd never much paid attention to before. Hormone conversations were like high school trigonometry, even when I tried to rehash them later, with Loren. I understood the theorems in class, but failed during homework to reconjure even a remote, working logic.

"Huh," Dr. Walla said, when I told her about the tanning. "Interesting."

Such was the tone for her responses these days—contemplative, elliptical. When I asked Dr. Walla about the reliability of localized radiotherapy, she'd said that Gamma Knife "*should* dissolve the residual tumor. But there's always that chance that it might not. . . . " On the experimental batch of chemicals I'd been preparing my bloodstream to handle: " . . . and if Sandostatin doesn't work to regulate your GHRH, we may have to try this other, newer treatment of daily injections that you can do at home. It's not on the market yet, but we'll get you on it if we *need* to. . . ." I'd even brought up the bottoming out at Mark McKiernan's wedding in the hope of a concrete explanation. "You *were* out of shape from bed rest, which was likely the major issue," she said. "But you say you had numbness? High thyroid can lead to anxiety attacks, but your thyroid dosages were fine if not low at the time, so numbness *shouldn't* have been a problem. . . ."

Given the rareness of my illness, I should have assumed no answer would be simple, that there was nothing left to be guaranteed. Dr. Walla, for her part, was figuring me out, too. But it wasn't easy to live as an equation in midsolution. I grew mildly paranoid about what might be the next surprise issue, hyperalert to my new rhythms, overconvinced of their severity, never sure what was hormone-related and what were just plain old body tics. Following a prolonged, swirling headache one evening, Loren and I debated for hours about returning to the ER, fearing a resurgence of the tumor, maybe another rupture—*if it still aches at 10:45, we'll call Dr. Walla and head in*—but then, thankfully, the pain faded. The skin on one of my left knuckles grew oddly callused, flaky and irritated, and because *acromegalics have hardened skin, and this callus is new, which might mean the tumor is growing back,* I brought it to Dr. Walla's attention at once ("Your levels are fine," she said. "Eczema, maybe?"). Weird growth on my lower earlobe? Nope, no tumor. Sebaceous cyst. Pop it with a pin. *Voila.* And now: tanning, or not tanning, or not being able to produce a tan.

"That's not something we can control," Walla said, and she was right. I know this now. There was nothing to be done about the MSH. It was a loss, and a very small one, relatively. But still: I wanted consolation. Instead Dr. Walla did what she knew how to, which was to remove a syringe from its package and dip it into a clear vile of Sandostatin, a time-released, hefty swirl of chemicals to be delivered piecemeal to my bloodstream over the course of five weeks from a needle so large it needed to plunge into the fleshiest, fattiest patch of my body: my pale, flat ass.

"Right side or left?" she asked.

Then I was belly flat on her exam table, pants around my thighs.

I'd been thinking for weeks about this radio interview I'd heard, with a man who'd unknowingly stopped producing testosterone, who'd gone without it for something like four months. He sounded a decade or two older than me, and spoke very eloquently about the experience, describing it as a life without desire that turned him into a droning robot who couldn't "distinguish between what is and isn't interesting." Testosterone triggers our carnal and social impulses—hunger, aggression, confidence—and without it he cared nothing about his aspirations, the food he ate, or the people he met. It gave him what he called "the most literal possible understanding of the world." Anything he saw, he summed up in one sentiment: *That is beautiful.* Bricks in walls, weeds in the sidewalk, they all became things he revered with "complete dispassion" and "objectivity," as though his world, at its simplest terms, was beautiful by default.

Every day at the bathroom sink as I counted my hormones out in my hand, it was hard not to grow curious about what I could realistically do without. Dr. Walla's assistant, Errol, had warned me (very vaguely) never to lapse on my cortisol dosages, that the body forms such a vigorous bond with it that going off the medication in any abrupt way could cause something irreparable, though he never said what, even when I pressed him ("It would just be very bad").

And I'd discovered, unfortunately, the dangers of not taking levothyroxine. The role of that medication was to step in for the signals no longer coming from my pituitary and impart my bloodstream with the T_4 hormones it needed for standard thyroid function—which assists brain fluidity, body temperature, muscle strength, metabolism. Without it, my doctors warned, the body and bloodstream breakdowns would occur quickly, with results ranging from the mundane (swollen ankles) to the frighteningly bizarre (eyebrow loss). There were times where my prescription renewals would lapse—my lax pharmacy waiting sometimes more than a week to verify refills with Dr. Walla—and during those days I slipped, almost unnoticeably, into darkly tiresome spells that I wouldn't realize until I was fully in them. I lost focus. Random pains pulsed through my back, hands, and legs. My muscles dripped heavy from my bones. I felt bruised, deep beneath the skin. Walking up stairs became almost impossible, and, depending on the lag—home from work, blurred, calling the pharmacy hourly to check on the prescriptions—so did getting out of bed. (Eyebrows, however, thankfully intact.)

But the one hormone no one mentioned anything about was testosterone. Of all my medications it seemed the least essential, and easily the most annoying. For the first months I spent my mornings in the bathroom with Loren's hairdryer to my arm, waiting for that thick, smelly gel to dry. On mornings where I was running too late for the hairdryer, I spent the rest of the day peeling off the sleeve of my shirt that had clung to the skin of my shoulder, the tiny flakes of medical ash shaking off, dandruff-like, onto my pant legs, my keyboard at work. While my cortisol and levothyroxine were tremendously cheap (ten dollars for both), even with my new, NY-based insurance through the educational publisher, AndroGel prescriptions still ran sixty dollars a pop. There was no way around it. And if it was a matter of libido, there had been no drop off in the year since my diagnosis, Loren and I using the few hours we had together each week to wear as few clothes as possible. Even the sterility it purportedly granted me—the very thing Loren and I liked best about the arrangement—was specious and unreliable. Earlier in the year Loren had toyed with the idea of going off birth control entirely for the first time since high school. It was a prospect she looked forward to, if only to remove the nagging regularity of it. But when I brought it up with Dr. Walla, she said she was "not sure that's the smartest idea," then, as with everything else, her reasoning became lost to either a lack of helpful detail or, just as likely, my inability to grasp whatever details there were.

Shortly after my first Sandostatin shot, and against her protestations (which seemed, in retrospect, disconcertingly mild),

I told Dr. Walla that I no longer felt I needed the testosterone, that my youth somehow overcompensated for my hormonal empty tank. I suppose I felt that was true, but that wasn't the only reason. A year in, I was so tired of trying to gauge what was happening in my blood, in my bones, on my face, in my hands, in my reflection, of seeing or feeling one thing and being told another—months and months of that frustrating swing between paranoia and the rebuke of it—that after hearing that radio show, something clicked, and I thought, *Dispassionate, objective beauty: I think I'm ready for that.*

I anticipated a guttural wiping-away, a reduction of what had become my life's ambient clatter since the diagnosis, similar to what I'd heard from the man on the radio. I hoped that the world might look different somehow, that its colors would augment. And things did change, but with the force of a feather duster. It took a week or two off testosterone for me to fully notice, but there emerged a slow muffle, an obstruction of volume, as though my daily life spoke to me with its hand covering its mouth. My morning commute to the children's publisher was a frantic gauntlet of elbows and sidesteps and jockeying for position on subway trains, a clamor for personal space that sometimes shook me up to the point where I arrived at work with gritted teeth and clenched knuckles. After just a few weeks of no testosterone, I felt loosened, easily pulled along by the swift current of the city. I wasn't completely without desire, but there was a relaxed matter-of-factness to my drive that I didn't have before.

Everything meant less, or seemed to. There was a detached whisper to the whole experiment. My senses seemed in pantomime. Since I'd moved to New York, I'd walked around my Brooklyn neighborhood unable to avoid staring at the roundest parts of all the gorgeous women who passed me, with their quick strides and their model frames and their lush, important-sounding voices. But without T there was only the empty re-enactment of lust. I saw them as women I would stare at, if I cared to. I'd think: *Well, that's the type of woman I know I find attractive.* Before, I couldn't escape the ways Loren's sly beauty and confidence pulled me after her with a sharp, carnal hunger. But off T, I responded only to the sense-memory of those things. I operated with strange, romantic nostalgia. She'd dismantle the flimsy logic of some neocon investment banker during a bar-room argument, or she'd throw her bare leg across my mid-section while in bed, and I'd think, plainly: *I know that this is one of the many reasons I fell in love with you.*

With no T it was as though I were cataloging life as I lived it. Whereas before I'd thought of myself as a hothead given to dramatic, cantankerous mood swings, now I found myself calm-headed during heavy deadline pushes at work, or flippant if, say, an editor at my trivia job dropped some comments into a feedback session that cut a little too personal. People began referring to me as "Zen" and "deadpan."

"You're so *laid back*," was the one I always liked to hear.

It affected how I saw myself, too. Before, a glimpse in the mirror at the wrong angle had sent me into a spiral of confusion and self-pity—*it's there, right there in my face, I'm Andre, fuck.*

Without T, it wasn't that I no longer cared what I looked like, but that I was incapable of feeling like it mattered. *Your temples are caved in now, maybe,* I'd say while looking at my reflection, which I'd become so tired of seeing, so tired of trying to interpret. No T meant there was no interpretation at all, and more importantly, no complication in the way I felt about that fact of what I now saw, the clarity of shape. I wasn't even me. Just some guy.

Fat hands. Chiseled. Whatever.

And that worked for me. For a while, anyway.

My mother was in a hospital bed in a hospital room and I was in a chair next to it. My brother and father were in chairs too, all of us watching the local sports report from Steelers training camp that played on the TV in the top corner of the recovery room. It profiled the team's offensive prospects that year, which, following a deep, heartbreaking playoff run last fall—one I'd watched with Ethan and Leigh in Steelers-themed bars in Hell's Kitchen, wearing a T-shirt with a photo of a donkey that read IF YOU AREN'T A STEELERS FAN YOU MUST BE A HUGE JACKASS—were, admittedly, very good. My mother, a pathologically critical fan who bickered from each game's first incomplete pass through to its end, even thought so. We had a new quarterback named Tommy Maddox, someone who until last season had been well out of the league, working as an insurance salesman. As she had with Terry Bradshaw and Joe Montana (who was never a Steeler, but went to high school in Pittsburgh), my mother had hatched a tremendous crush on Maddox. He was, as she put it, a "cutie-

cutie." My father, brother, and I weren't sold on him. We asserted with trumped-up authority that Maddox and his "quick release" meant the Steelers would likely move to "a pass-first offense," how our offensive line wasn't built for that, how our cornerbacks "would have to play much tighter" in the event of a shootout, which was not "our game"—none of us had ever played football, ever—and my mother, eyes half closed, bandages along her arm, still weary from the anesthesia, would cut in.

"Yes," she'd say, "but he's a cutie-cutie."

It was July, and my mother's fourth stent procedure had gone the way the previous ones had: a mildly intense invasion of an artery followed by brief observation and release back into the world. For all the histrionics of last Christmas, my mother seemed unfazed now that it was over, almost relieved. I, too, had imagined it going horribly, and swelled with a familiar kind of worry. But now I was a month off T, thankful for that same calm, alien distance that I'd had for everything else. There was none of the morose anxiousness that had bound me to my mother's previous procedures, no gurgle of worry and dread in my gut as I neared home. My brother and father wanted some food, they said, and headed off to the hospital cafeteria, leaving my mother, me, and the sports report.

"That's a nice gift you gave your father," she said once they were gone. Her eyes were still closed.

My father's birthday happened within weeks of my mother's latest stent procedure, so in a weak attempt at milestone consolidation I'd given him a bronze Zippo lighter to add to his collection. Proud of the swell of work I'd had in recent months, particularly the magazine gigs, I'd had the Zippo engraved on one side with the words A PROFESSIONAL JOURNALIST BOUGHT ME THIS. In the days that I was home I'd been saying that about everything.

"We're ordering pizza," my brother had said the night before, "what toppings should we get?"

"Look," I told him. "As a professional journalist, I recommend you get half pepperoni, half sausage and olives."

"You guys want to watch a DVD?" my father asked later.

"As a professional journalist," I told him, "I suggest you avoid *Daredevil.*"

And so on.

So when my mother mentioned the lighter in the hospital, I told her I felt my father might like the gesture, that, as a professional journalist, I felt he'd get a kick out of it.

"Well," my mother said, eyes still closed in that hospital bed. "Maybe one day you'll be able to get him a Zippo that says 'a *successful* journalist bought me this.'"

If she'd said something like that at home, on shared ground, I'd have returned fire. I wouldn't have been able to stop myself. "Someone in this family has to succeed at *something,*" I maybe, probably (definitely), would have said, then launched into a tirade of bitter, chip-on-the-shoulder fury.

It had happened so many times before, my mother keying in on a situation I'd been subtly proud of, then leveling it, and me, with a single comment. Shortly before I graduated college, with Loren in tow, she'd offered to take me shopping for what she called "adult clothes"—biz-casual wear I'd later sweat through on the way to my job interviews. She drove Loren and me to a strip in Pittsburgh with shops and restaurants and metered parking in nearby lots, and while we went on to have a surprisingly un-tense few hours, when we first parked the car my mother realized she had no change, and neither did I, and neither did Loren, so my mother offered to break a dollar at the nearby drugstore, which she did.

That was, it seems even now as I write it, the least interesting detail of an otherwise pleasant afternoon, capable of zero dissection. Yet weeks later, at my parents' house, my mother on the couch, the following conversation took place:

MY MOTHER: "That was a nice time with Loren a few weeks back."

ME: "Yeah, it was great."

MY MOTHER: "That was funny how none of us had any change for the meter."

ME: "Yeah? Was it?"

MY MOTHER [*sips iced Pinot from a mammoth glass*]: "Yeah, that was funny."

ME: "If you say so?"

MY MOTHER [*laughing*]: "You know what *I* think?"

ME: "What's that."

MY MOTHER: "*I* think Loren had change. For the meter."

ME: "—"

MY MOTHER: "*I* think she had change, and *I* think she didn't want to give it to me. Because she's cheap."

ME: "She flies me out to New York every month, Mom. I pay for none of that—"

MY MOTHER: "She's fucking *cheap.*"

And I lost it on her.

The year before, after I'd told my parents I couldn't, while they were at work, wait at their home for furniture to be delivered because I was slated to interview a band at a press junket for a page-long feature in the alt-weekly I wrote for, my mother called me at 1:00 A.M. and accused me of being an ungrateful son. After a protracted screaming fight, I left a message on my editor's voicemail, ditched the junket—the band's single would conquer the Billboards within weeks— and spent the morning, angry and alone in their living room, waiting for two guys and a couch. I never got another assignment from the alt-weekly.

There were more instances like that. But I was not blameless. I knew how to deflate her, too. My freshman year in college, my mother had agreed to drive the four-plus hours down to Ohio to pick me up for a weekend trip home to attend the funeral of one of Jeff Stibner's ex-girlfriends, who'd died swiftly from a resurgence of cancer we'd all thought she'd outrun. My mother had gotten lost on the way to my college, somewhere in the curved roads of West Virginia, and arrived two hours later than expected, exhausted, wanting a break before the four-plus-hour drive back.

"No. You're fucking late," was the first thing I said when she arrived, and she burst into tears then whipped her keys at me.

My mother and I had trained for these kinds of interactions for years—*hit me, hit me back*—but now, in the recovery room, of course I would say nothing, do nothing. Current health predicament aside, I knew my mother and I weren't on shared ground. This hospital room was my mother's ground. I was part of her universe of illness, and in any other mindset, with different hormones churning through me, I probably would have done the only thing I could get away with: a quiet, swift dismissal of myself from that room, a silent *fuck off* she would probably never register.

Instead I took mental inventory, cold and operational like I'd been doing almost instinctively for weeks. *I know that this is my mother, and this is What We Do.* It permitted me to unwind myself from the moment, to see that remark, its origin and in-tention, as absurd, useless. It was—all of it—*funny.*

"*Wow*, Mom," I said, chuckling. And that was it.

We sat wordless after that, the sports report detailing how the Pirates hadn't won a game in nearly a month, the sports-caster's voice now filling the worn air. And my non-reaction, and the silence after, left enough space between us for some-thing new to happen.

"I don't know why I just said that," my mother finally said. "I'm sorry, Mike. I don't know why I just said that."

Toward the end of the summer, a disaffected, sarcastic copy-editor named Kyle—a guy I'd been to a few happy hours with, but didn't know terribly well—came to my desk with a prop-osition. He wanted my protection. Kyle wore tennis shoes each day, and was tall and lanky. He looked very much like I did before I started cortisol and put on weight. He had a thick brush burn across his left eyebrow, and small cuts on his chin, as if someone had scraped his face across a patch of gravel. He'd been living with a roommate, he said, an insane-seeming person who'd threatened his life on a few occasions and had most recently been stalking him outside of work. They'd gotten into an awkward fistfight in the street in front of his apartment the night before, so he'd spent the night on his girlfriend's couch.

"I need to get my shit out of my apartment," he said. "*Aye-sapp.*"

"Sounds like it."

"I'm pretty sure my roommate's going to try to kill me when I do," he said. "I mean like, actually kill me. If I go alone." He said that though he "didn't want to put me out," I'd "really be doing him a solid" by going with him to his apartment on the far end of Brooklyn to help him move that night.

"You're a pretty big dude," he said. "You look like you can scrap. He won't mess with you."

Four months earlier, this might have been a difficult decision. It was the first time I'd ever been considered an asset to a rumble, and I was flattered. Before the No T Experiment, I might have been clouded by the compliment and convinced myself that I was how Kyle saw me, someone who could "scrap." I might have ridden the R train to the outskirts of Brooklyn with a guy I barely knew, adopting some ill-fitting, bouncer-like façade of frat-boy toughness while my hands trembled with fear and apprehension. And I'm sure I would have had my face stomped by someone who seemed to be, in Kyle's description, an unhinged, human cannibal.

How much of it had to do with testosterone? Maybe none at all. But I was able to quickly parse the situation and trim it down to the essentials. Unlike the man on the radio, I never had a *that is beautiful* moment. Bricks and weeds looked like bricks and weeds. Instead, each moment had its own particular, simplistic deliberation. *That's the type of woman I know I find attractive. This is how I know I love you.*

As I had for four months now, I wondered why I couldn't feel things more deeply or widely, or why my personal default couldn't put a poetic, *that is beautiful* gloss on everything. Was it just my age? The man on the radio, perhaps middle-aged, was viewing everything in retrospect, looking backward. The beauty he described was the result of a decades-long, sub-conscious struggle with desire, and he'd come to it after years of internal debate. I was twenty-five now, but maybe my palate was still too clean for that kind of verdict. Maybe all of that cold cataloging, those scattered, simple reductions, were my way to begin taking stock; to develop a vocabulary for the man I was becoming.

There were some surprises, but in many cases it turned out I was the same person I'd been from day one. Regardless of how I looked now or how I appeared to carry myself, I was and always had been someone who tried hard to avoid conflict, who got my ass kicked when I didn't. So when Kyle asked me to be his muscle, the only thing I thought, with as little passion as possible, was *that sounds like a fucking terrible idea.*

"That's no good, Kyle," I told him, "but I'm definitely not your man here."

That weekend I tried to explain everything to Loren. On a late Saturday morning, the part of the day when the body's T levels are at their highest, we lay in bed with mussed hair and bad breath, her forehead pressed against my shoulder. I talked in circles: about Kyle's roommate, the surprising gift of self-clarity, the calm of detachment, and the great value of having the "most literal possible understanding of the world."

She peeked her head up at me.

"That's great, baby," she said. "Think we might be able to have sex one of these days?"

Flat on my back, I looked down to see her soft leg stretched across my stomach. It felt like a leg. She swiped her fingernails lightly up and down my chest. They felt like fingernails.

She kissed my neck, and it felt wet.

Four months ago, I thought, she wouldn't have even gotten this far. My time off T may have allowed me to switch off my desire and everything that came with it, but what if the binding to that catalog—what held those pages together at their spine—were the small, shared fortunes of the privately familiar? For as lucky as I felt to hear those solitary, whispered contemplations—for those months of new, ethereal me-ness—I'd apparently forgotten about the beauty of feeling beyond thinking, chasing after your most trusted impulses.

"How long has it been?" I asked.

"Two months," she said. Then she held up two fingers in a V, about an inch away from my nose, and repeated, "Two. Whole. Months."

That was when I called in a prescription refill, and stopped work immediately on the No T Experiment.

CH. 15

GAME

Sometimes it happened on the sidewalk, or in bookstores, or at restaurants, but mostly it happened on the subway. I'd glimpse the heft of someone's hand, or the plumpness in the fold of someone's finger, or the lack of it in the shapeless contour of a forearm in my sightline, dangling from a rail. I'd notice a pair of feet with a certain proportion, a brow. The jawlines were the easiest to catch: the angles, how wide they were, how long across them people's pursed mouths stretched.

They've got it too, I'd think, piqued yet heartsunk. Then I'd spend the rest of my time on the train, pulling hard around the curves of the uptown A, the Brooklyn-bound F, stopping myself from studying them further, or sizing the person up more than I already had. But I couldn't help imagining composite realities for the people I'd just inducted, unknowingly, into the posse of acromegalics. The calm-looking man in the cardigan, with the heavy head and the sunken temples, his fat, GH-stuffed fingers clutched around the handle of a beaten leather briefcase, perhaps en route to his job as a database systems specialist at the public library—maybe he never finds out. Maybe he lives to fifty-eight, entirely oblivious, saying the word "Boolean" in an assuring, no-big-deal way to people looking for research support, until he bursts in the chest, like André Roussimoff did, from an enlarged heart. Or maybe the woman standing near the door with pulled-back hair and crooked smile *knows* she's got something but isn't sure what, or why she can't sleep, or why she's sweating hard right now, not moving, through the spandex of that gym outfit, well after she's left the elliptical.

"Him. *Look*," I'd whisper to Loren when we rode the trains together.

"You can see, right in his hands."

"The face. And the skin tags on the neck."

It was as though I was a birdwatcher.

"Shouldn't you be *telling* these people?" Loren once asked.

"What do I say?" I said. "Hi, person, I noticed your enormous hands and caveman head, and I just wanted to let you know that you probably have a ball of tumor smothering your pituitary gland right now, causing untold havoc to your bloodstream and skin and bones. Tell me: how've you been sleeping?" And what if by strange chance they *had* been diagnosed already, I told her, and here I was, some guy, approaching them in public, around people with eyes, not just telling them what they've already known and have been taking pills or getting shots to combat, but worse: confirming for that person—who may or may not have spent the same amount of time inspecting themselves as I had, wondering how frightfully their features were regarded by the many, many eyes that fell upon them—that, above all, they *looked diagnosable*. I understood too much about that complicated fear to confirm it for anyone else.

That's what I told Loren, and it sounded noble, chip-shouldered, and respectful leaving my lips. I thought so when I said it, like I'd won something. The Insight Awards. But what I didn't say, probably because I couldn't say it to myself yet, was, *plus: If I told all those people, I wouldn't get to have the condition all to myself.*

CH. 16

WHAT OKAY FEELS LIKE NOW

*M*onths passed, many of them, then, one day, Loren and I were getting married. It was June of 2004, more than a year after Gamma Knife, and we were in bed. It had been two years since we'd moved in together, and it had become clear over that time that our aversion to marriage was a relic of a far less logical era. Loren's student status meant she had no health coverage, and I'd grown paranoid about the obvious pitfalls of that predicament. Then more practicalities emerged: taxes, power of attorney in the event of incapacitation, prime beneficiary of insurance, a living will. Loren and I found each other considering wedlock first playfully, then less so. For weeks I'd leaked hints to my parents and close friends—to whom I'd been unabashedly obnoxious for years about staying unwedded—that we'd "begun thinking

about it." Then, on a nondescript evening in June, before falling away to sleep as our window AC unit hummed:

"Look, it makes sense," I said.

Loren exhaled, laughed and said, "God-*dammit*," and we
went to work immediately on a new set of terms.

The first person I told was Dr. Walla. She and I were well into
the bimonthly Sandostatin LAR injections, well into waiting
for one disaster to end and another to begin.

"We're thinking in two months," I said.

"That—no," she said. "*Not* a good idea. Weddings are stressful events," she said.

Dr. Walla opened her desk drawers and ducked into file cabi-
nets. For those with healthy hormones, she explained, stress
sparks the pituitary to brew adrenocorticotropic hormone,
which directs the adrenal gland to flood the body with cortisol,
a steroid that transports nutrients, regulates the immune system, combats body inflammation, and tells the liver to produce
blood sugar. But cortisol's prime role is as a stress and anxiety
combatant, secreted during our fight-or-flight response, which
means it's impossible to predict when our bodies will need
it most. Without it, Dr. Walla said, intense stress could lead to
no fight-or-flight response at all—sharp fatigue, plummeting
blood pressure, deranged cognition—and could even trigger
what she called "adrenal crisis," an internal overload of the
body's biorhythms, a certain of-the-moment paralysis that
might, if unchecked, lead to circulatory collapse or hypo-
glycemia, which would wash over one's body like a stroke.

Dr. Walla insisted that I double my cortisol dosage in the run-up to the wedding day, "or any other stress-heavy event, for that matter." She slid a sheet of paper across her desk like a tarot card. On it was a space labeled MEDICAL CONDITION where Walla had written the words *Adrenal Insufficiency*. Under MEDICATIONS: *Steroids*. The sheet featured various styles of jewelry; some of it gold-like, some silver, decorative amulets all engraved with a familiar, snake-rounded staff.

It was an order form for MedicAlert bracelets.

"It's just, if you get into an accident," Walla said, "or any other situation where your body can't cope, and you can't communicate—" and I'd like to say I thought of the previous Christmas, standing frozen against the wall watching my mother wail, hands numb, unable to move, or of Mark McKiernan's wedding, or of lifeguarding, of blasting that whistle, launching, reflexively, after sinking humans.

But the truth is, I thought only of my daily schedule. By now I considered myself a pro at stress. In the year since Gamma Knife, Loren had moved from a job she hated to a graduate program she loved, and I worked every job under the sun. I was good at it now. I knew its rhythms, and liked the kind of exhaustion it produced. I felt like I was contributing, like I was *living*. The topic of stress had come to be the centerpiece of nearly all my conversations with people: how much we'd been working, how little we saw of our significant others, how tired we were. This was our language now, our means for conversational barter. How could stress suddenly be a grave concern when it was the only currency I knew?

And besides: Loren and my decision to marry had been made entirely with "no stress" in mind. Not just for us, but for everyone involved. Our wedding would be small and fast, we decided, like tearing off a bandage. Labor Day weekend, in the city, and unlike the cash-heavy ceremonies we'd been party to every summer since college, there would be no planning, no arranging of tables, no satellite events, and no imposition. City Hall, immediate families only, followed by a celebratory dinner at a decent restaurant. We'd send a plain, non-intrusive announcement to everyone we knew and be done with it. Then we'd return to the comforts of the more familiar brand of stress we'd already immersed ourselves in.

I nodded, turned the MedicAlert form over in my hands. There weren't just bracelets. There were necklaces, shoelace tags, and watches with steel-linked wristbands, the same kind my father had collected for years as welcome gifts from union organization seminars he'd attended.

"You don't have to wear the *bracelet*," Walla said. "Did you see the dog tags? Those are pretty cool."

The MedicAlert form took up residence in the bottom of my shoulder bag.

Days later I went back to Pittsburgh, where my mother intercepted my wedding news with some of her own. She, my father, my brother, and I were on the porch again, three of us smoking again, when she announced with exasperation that her doctors had discovered two more obstructed arteries: one in her neck and another running up the length of her left leg.

She propped her head up on the arm of her chair and held her fingertips to her forehead, nostrils leaking smoke. Her eyes closed for long, deliberate stretches as she explained that both arteries were perilously clogged, in several key places, and that she'd been scheduled for a dual procedure at the end of the month. My father, brother, and I had by now adjusted to the speedy, near-outpatient rhythm of her stent procedures, which typically had her up and mobile within days. But this one was substantial, she said, abnormally extensive, and likely required a weeks- or maybe months-long healing process before she might walk again at full gait.

"Those are the breaks," my mother said, then put both of her hands up in the air. No one spoke for what felt like five minutes.

"Beats what I got," I said. "Loren and I were thinking of getting married in September. Fuck *that*."

My mother smiled, congratulated me, and tried hard to pour a new mood into the air. I'd hinted at the decision for months, but she seemed genuinely surprised. She asked about plans, why now, were we pregnant (*nope, not possible, never possible*), then bloomed into a quick and powerful excitement about how Loren—whom for years she'd seemed increasingly ambivalent about—would "be her daughter now."

"Mom, *no*," I said, laughing. "This wedding situation is *not* a big deal. Very much the opposite. It's almost kind of a joke." I told her we'd just decided this week, and that we hadn't told anyone yet, and that we'd push the date. Her "good health at the event" was far, far more important.

My mother's face grew stern. She flashed her jagged lower teeth.

"I *will be at my son's wedding*," she said.

"No one's saying you won't," I said. "I'm just saying the wedding can wait till you can be there in full force. Seriously—"

But it was too late. She'd already locked into a cadence, pulling away at that Marlboro and repeating herself in a softer, stricter tone that seemed in seconds no longer directed at anyone on that porch. Within a week my parents had reserved a room at a hotel four blocks from our apartment.

CH. 17

BEST MAN

Two days before our wedding I walked into a downtown Manhattan tavern to find Jeff Stibner—who eight years earlier had fished me from the bottom of a high school pool, then spread false news of my death to the entire student body—berating a bartender. It was Wednesday, 4:00 P.M., and Jeff was boldly unsober. He wore a blue flowered shirt, linen clamdiggers that hung wide over the knee, and stood upright at the bar, holding his bill and yelling, "I AM FROM HAWAII, YOU HAVE TO HOOK ME UP FOR THAT," to a stout, beer-pouring man who, I could tell, had already depleted his reserve of patience.

Over the phone, weeks before, Jeff had told me about inside information he'd gained from friends and coworkers: that Manhattan food service professionals—by virtue of some unspoken, island-bound brotherhood—gave healthy discounts to their counterparts from Honolulu, where Jeff had been waiting tables at an upscale steakhouse for the last two years. He'd arrived in New York that morning via a nonstop flight halfway across the earth and aimed, I assumed, to test the theory's validity.

Which, of course, was none.

"Aw, you know I'm just fucking with you, right, buddy?" Jeff said to the bartender, then flopped down a stack of cash.

The bartender refused to make eye contact.

"Hey," Jeff called out to him. "Hey man. HEY."

The bartender turned around. Jeff curled his fingers into loose horns and smiled.

"*Mahalo*, brother."

Jeff gripped my neck.

"Alright, this guy *definitely* wants to kick my ass a little bit," he said. "We should go. I am *fading*, and I"—now up a decibel, booming, pointing at the bartender—"NEED SOME COKE. FOR MY NOSE."

Jeff Stibner was in town because he wouldn't *not* be in town. Like many in our circles he'd heard our plans for a tiny, uncomplicated affair, registered those plans, then rejected them at once. Our immediate families would be there as designed, but Ethan the documentarian insisted on photographing us post-hitch. Loren's best friend Fay in Los Angeles—whom Loren hadn't seen since my tumor's rupture cut short her trip there two years earlier—not only arranged to fly across the country, but to bring a small team of friends and relatives in tow. A pack of our Pittsburgh-based friends from high school, we'd heard, were caravanning into the city for post-event festivities, none of which we planned or wanted or understood what to do with.

But it was the most generous, uniformly blatant ignorance Loren or I had ever witnessed, and we were left with little recourse but to honor and accept it. The trivia writers scheduled a wedding night party at a bar with torn secondhand couches. My Australian boss at the children's publisher had bought us a crystal bowl that would be, for many years, the nicest thing we owned. Days before the wedding I noticed my trivia-writing paycheck had inexplicably doubled, and when I asked my boss there about it he only said, "You're welcome, big guy." And Jeff Stibner, my closest friend throughout high school, college, and our respective moves away from Pittsburgh—which happened in tandem within a week of one another in 2002, and had gone only slightly better for him than for me—heard about our wedding, took a fat hunk of tips down to an actual, human travel agent and paid cash for a round-trip flight to what he now called, with zero irony, "the mainland."

Now we had to find "coke for his nose." I knew this because as we wove through the human tangle of Broadway to the subway platform and onto the 6 train, toward the large uptown apartment of Shawn Chipp—another mutual (and well off) Pittsburgh expat who'd arranged, though Loren and I begged otherwise, a Saturday celebration in his Upper East Side highrise—Jeff Stibner made it known to me and everyone in his vocal range that of the habits he'd picked up in recent years, "coke for my nose" was currently the most urgent.

Our wedding coincided with the Republican National Convention, held that year at Madison Square Garden. The event had infused the city with both an unwelcome dose of smug, white neocons and a nebulous fear of exploding invaders, which in turn triggered a flood of heightened security, most notably on the subways: two to three cops to a platform, maybe on foot, maybe hovering upright on pitiful Segways, and definitely proctoring the train cars. Jeff didn't care. For eleven stops and sixty city blocks he kept on. "HOW DO I GET SOME COKE FOR MY NOSE? CAN SOMEONE IN THIS CITY PLEASE TELL ME HOW TO GET SOME COKE FOR MY NOSE? I AM FROM HAWAII," and I moved from lecturing to laughter to resignation, until two officers entered our train car through the connecting door at the far end.

"Please, just let us get to Shawn's," I asked Jeff, and for the next few stops he receded to a goofy mumble, joking about my work pants, calling them "slacks." As the police walked past where we sat and into the next car, we finally entered into a fine silence. My eyes lowered to the floor. I figured Jeff had passed out, but then I heard the snare of a lighter, looked left, and saw that on a fully occupied 6 train, with two stops remaining on our ride and two policemen just a car over, Jeff Stibner had gone and lit himself a Camel Light.

There was no coke for Jeff's nose. There was no coke for

anyone's nose, Shawn Chipp said. On account of the Republicans and the police-state fervor, his network of dealers and delivery services had suspended all activity save for reasonable marijuana purchases. So that, Shawn said, would have to do. (I certainly had my vices, but drugs—at least the kind of drugs Jeff Stibner preferred—were no longer among them. Drugs turned me manic and insular, fixated and paranoid, and after my rupture I discovered there were certain things I did not want to be manic or insular or fixated or paranoid about.)

While we waited for the delivery, Jeff fell asleep on the hardwood in front of Shawn Chipp's couch. In the adjoining computer room, Shawn and I searched for bars or restaurants fitting for tomorrow night's bachelor party which, again, I wanted little to do with. Shawn was a real estate developer, one of Jeff's college friends whom I'd known in Pittsburgh but not well. Why he was so insistent on facilitating my wedding was beyond me. He was linked to money through his family and—like a friend-starved new neighbor with the only in-ground pool on the block—was overeager to share it. He'd arrived in the city earlier that year, then extended Loren and me constant invites to weekends at his parents' Connecticut house and to thumping, club-type places featuring badly dancing people in suits. I'd arrive in jeans and sneakers, drink a seventeen-dollar whiskey, let Shawn pay for it, then return to my natural habitat of sad, quiet dives near my apartment to meet up with Loren or Ethan or the trivia writers. Shawn and I were trying to find a happy medium for the bachelor party when we heard the front door open and shut, the clack of high heels. Then Shawn's live-in girlfriend—a spritely, gravel-voiced publicist—knocked lightly on the computer room's door.

"Why is there a man sleeping on his back on our living room floor?" she asked. "And why does he have a massive erection?"

In the cab back Jeff slept, head pressed against the window, rattling out snorts and wheezes. It was a type of night I never grew numb to while I lived in New York. The city had eased into a soothing rev of motion and light, sputter and sound—all of it so typical, so easy—a soft, tickling beauty that dismantled its cliché. As we crossed the Brooklyn Bridge I tapped Jeff, then punched him, then punched him a little harder. When he woke I pointed to the glow of the monuments over the river—*just look, man*—but he could only muster a grunt.

Once Jeff Stibner finished vomiting in my bathroom, I opened the medicine cabinet and prepared the next day's crop of hormones, set them on the sink. One pill of levothyroxine (125 mcg), one packet of AndroGel (5 mg). For my cortisol I took out one pill (10 mg), and, like always, broke off an extra half-pill for the low-cortisone P.M. hours (5 mg), then quickly decided—with my mother, father, and brother set to arrive in the morning, or maybe in the late afternoon, not sure, they hadn't decided yet, they'd call whenever they got on the road, did I need them to bring anything, was I sure?—to go ahead and double it.

CH. 18

WEDDING

On the morning of my mother's dual stent procedure I visited two different care units. It was a month before my wedding, and I was back in Pittsburgh. My father, the Ambassador of Information, had given my brother and me the wrong hospital location—though to be fair, my mother had by now occupied nearly every cardiovascular wing in town—so we arrived at one and walked through the blue, clanging hallways, pestering admin staffers, playing *Have You Seen My Mother?* until my father called and said, "Whoops," after which we drove across town to another, smaller, more drab-looking building.

During my mother's procedures I now simmered with guilt about the storied majesty of the medical buildings I had access to. I was thankful for those moments when, lying pants-down on the exam table waiting for my Sandostatin shot, I could peek past Dr. Walla's dripping AC unit, past the rooftop reservoirs, to the morning shimmer of the Hudson. Pittsburgh's hospitals were low brick compounds surrounded by folds of Pittsburgh itself, which is to say parking lots full of minivans and lined with dead trees.

And just like in a movie—surgery visits are so much like dumb movies and television shows, infecting your fine, healthy concern with a bland, inauthentic template that turns everything more maddening and intolerable, homogenizing the very rich, very personal anxiety you've spent weeks mentally curating—we arrived in time to see my mother, eager surgeons and anesthetizers shoving her tiny, tube-woven body down the hallway on a gurney.

"I know, *I know*, I'm a dickhead," my father said regarding the mix-up, then for hours we resumed our standard rotations. Waiting room, cafeteria, coffee, parking lot cigarettes, gift shop, waiting room, card game, update. More blocked than we'd thought, more invasive than we'd planned. She's out now, doing fine and resting, she'll see you in a minute. Phone calls, phone calls, phone calls.

My mother looked *bad*. She was in a dim, windowless recovery dungeon in the ICU, a taupe haze over her, bed affixed with plinking monitors and wires that cut into her weak arms and legs and hung off to her sides like swamp vines. Hissing air tubes taped into her nose. Wide, white bandages curled around her neck, over her leg. She seemed gutted, maimed in some stark, irreparable manner. If my mother didn't look like death in that low, yellow room, she was at least its advertisement. My father walked to her bedside but—hesitant to disrupt her new, delicate machinery—quickly jammed his hands deep into his pockets. *Smooth move, Dad*, I thought, then realized it was in fact the *only* move, so I put my helpless, idiot hands in my pockets, too.

"I'm going to see you get *married*," my mother said, her voice a faint rasp, the skin on her lips cracked. She clicked her dry tongue between words. "I'm going to see you get married," she said, "and I'll get to see you have grandkids, I know it, I will. I'm going to be a good grandmother to two pretty little baby girls . . ."

When my family arrived in New York that September, the Thursday evening before my wedding, we fell into a symphony of passive aggression, hostility, and rote accommodation regarding when they arrived, where they stayed, and how, exactly, my mother would possibly participate in a wedding. She was just a month into a recovery her doctors had said "would take quite a while" to yield full mobility, still with long jet streams of fresh-looking scar streaking down her leg, running up from her collar bone. On all of these matters, my parents were sullen and confident, unwavering and resolute.

I was, for my part, an extraordinary asshole.

"Can we just *walk*? You know what? We're going to walk," I said. Loren had already left with her friends and mother for a bachelorette evening, and Jeff Stibner, Shawn Chipp, Ethan, Loren's brother, et al., had already begun whatever night they'd had planned at some dreaded place on the far end of the city (my cell phone rumbled with increasing frequency, calls and text messages that read things like WHERE ARE YOU, YOU TRE-MENDOUS BALL HAIR). I'd met my parents and brother at their hotel, checked them in, then informed them that I was "hungry," that I'd expected them "*way* earlier," and that we'd eat in downtown Brooklyn which—I showed them by pointing—was a short walk across the plaza. "*Right there*," I said. "There's a nice place with good pierogies, better than at home. You can see it from here. It's just like, *two blocks*—"

It took twenty minutes to cross the plaza. This is not an overstatement. My mother held my father's arm as, behind them, my brother and I shuffled—a word that seems, even now, far too generous a description—across the same flat area I covered in seconds each morning on my way to work. She was smoking with her free hand, a fifty-one-year-old woman moving in the most geriatric of increments, talking about the drive from Pittsburgh, their first since my tumor's rupture, but this time they'd taken Route 70 instead of the PA Turnpike, which was quicker and cheaper but had too many eighteen-wheelers, which made her nervous. The distance we covered couldn't have been more than four hundred yards. We stopped three times to rest.

"Are you serious with this?"

She apologized. Or I think she did. My father and brother joined together in a wordless no-reaction. I couldn't stop looking at her scars, raw and skin-thatched like they could split back open at any minute. I reexamined the next day's plans:

3:00 P.M. at City Hall, then photos immediately after at Battery Park, which was a mile away on foot. My mother had assured me repeatedly that this would be no obstacle. She felt good, she had told me, was exercising, responding well to medications, ready to "see my new daughter down the aisle," and my father had echoed her.

"So are we walking back?" I asked after dinner, standing in front of the restaurant, again pointing directly at their hotel, which my mother would stay in that night with my brother, then twenty and unable to enter bars. "Or do you want to flag a cab this time, with all these people, to go *two whole blocks*."

We cabbed.

My brother accompanied my mother to her hotel room then my father and I shot off to my bachelor party at a loud, crowded bar on the Upper East Side. Everyone had work the next day—who has a bachelor party on a Thursday?—and soon we were right back in a cab, my father, Jeff Stibner and I, en route to a corner spot a few blocks from my apartment, which I liked because it had no name, just a stencil on a plank of wood that read BAR.

My parents had always appreciated my friends, particularly Stibner. My mother liked to compare my crew to the folks she and my father had embedded themselves with in their youth. My parents, like Loren and me, had met in high school and remained in rugged tandem thereafter, and my mother seemed comforted by any hint of intergenerational symmetry. Jeff reminded her of someone somewhere. As for my father, he extended to each of my friends the same rough-knuckled affection he showed me. He took great pleasure in dropping my friends to the floor with the Connery-thumb, engaging in minor choke holds, half nelsons and—as he'd done with me since fifth grade—waking them from sleepovers with a cold glass of water to the face. Stibner was the first who thought to retaliate (gut smacks, nipple twists, forehead art while he slept on the couch), which my father respected. Out of that respect grew a juvenile shorthand between the three of us—my father's nickname for Stibner: "Meatball"—and at BAR we wasted no time resuming it.

Jeff bought shots and flicked the back of my father's head or gave him wet willies after bathroom breaks. I calmed down, discussed the cab route to City Hall with my father—*straight shot across the bridge, super easy.* There was a sand bucket outside BAR that the three of us used to play basketball with our cigarette butts. I talked about politics, which my father hates. Jeff talked about Hawaii's surplus of Spam, which my father loves. My father told a story about once meeting Jack Lambert in a bar and being frightened. I asked him if he wrote about it in his "secret feelings journal," then Jeff called him a "labia," and my father thumbed us both in the ribs until we nearly stumbled over. We were drunk, but it felt okay now, this wedding thing, and I wanted to say that to my father as he and I smoked out on the curb later, alone this time—the anemic 2:30 A.M. street traffic, just a few hovering, eager cabs—but saw instead that he was weeping.

"Sorry," my father said. "Things are fucked up."

Which was all he said.

"It's been a hard few years."

Which was all I said.

Stibner came out and the three of us patted each other's shoulders, then decided it was best to get my father a cab. But when I opened the door to one, Jeff tapped my shoulder and pointed to my father, who'd toppled back-flat on the sidewalk, face to the sky, laughing in a light, easy hoot, as though he'd rather be no place else.

At 2:38 P.M. the next afternoon I stood in the drop-port of Shawn Chipp's high rise, booze-sweating in a black wool suit, talking uselessly about dividends and investments with the Russian taxi driver whose task it was to get four people seventy-one city blocks in less than twenty-two minutes. He was my age, twenty-six, and wore a sleeveless T-shirt and a backward ball cap. I knew his name and secondary occupation because it was embossed on his business card, which he'd just given me: ALEC TULEV, INVESTOR & ENTREPRENEUR.

"My father and I"—Alec was in partnership with his father, I'd already learned, based out of their home office in Queens—"grasp the market fluck-tyoo-*way*-shuns quite well, sir," he said. "So when you and your wife are ready, I would love to link you with some investment options that would be ex-*tur*-reem-ly valuable to a young couple like yourselves."

The meter was running. My hands were in my pockets, then checking the time on my phone, then back in my pockets again.

"I appreciate that," I told him, "but I have to *get* a wife first."

We were waiting for Jeff Stibner, who'd arrived in New York City with seven Hawaiian shirts of varying hues and designs, but not one suit for the ceremony and dinner, scheduled at a fine-enough waterfront restaurant immediately following photographs. He'd arranged the night before to borrow one from Loren's brother, an agreeable guy with whom Jeff shared the same broad build. But for reasons that remain unclear, Loren's brother couldn't deliver the suit to my apartment in Brooklyn, where Jeff stayed, which would have meant a short trip across the Brooklyn Bridge to City Hall. Instead Loren's brother requested that I bring Jeff Stibner to Shawn Chipp's, where he'd been staying—over eight miles for proper attire—after which he, his girlfriend, Jeff and I would travel six-plus miles back downtown to the doors of City Hall.

Jeff and I began flagging cabs at around 1:30, but—and I blame the Republicans for this—we didn't find Alec Tulev or his open cab until shortly after 2:00 which, if you factor in a wardrobe change, puts you in a drop-port of a high rise, talking market fluctuations with a Russian less than a half-hour before your wedding.

"Twenty minutes, Alec," I said when I saw our people pour out of the lobby. "You feel all right about that?"

He shrugged. "We will see."

Alec was skilled at efficient road choices and late-second traffic maneuvers, and we didn't get jammed up until the lower basin, just a block or two from City Hall, meaning we'd have to hoof it at 2:57. I considered the trip an astounding success—

even yelled out, hands raised, "Victory!"—until, as we were about to hop out, I mentally reviewed the plans (*meet Loren at 3:00, right in front of the metal detectors*) and realized we'd made a near-grave mistake.

"Stibner," I said, turned around, speaking low. I was in front, next to Alec. Jeff, Loren's brother, and his girlfriend sat in back. "Do you have on your person anything that might endanger our chances of passing through security?"

Jeff's face went blank.

"Yes," he said. "Yes I do."

"You have to get rid of it."

"It was very expensive."

"You have to get rid of it," I said, "or stay outside until we're done."

"ALEC TULEV," Jeff said.

Alec snapped to attention.

"You get high?"

"No," said Alec. "No sir, I am sorry."

"You sure?"

"No sir, you are nice to ask, and I am very sorry, but these are working hours."

It was 2:58 and the fare was close to sixty dollars. Jeff passed a tiny glass bowl through the partition—one he'd bought the previous day at an overpriced paraphernalia table at Union Square—and dropped it on the seat. I handed over four twenty-dollar bills, then Jeff slapped a near ounce of two-day-old cannabis on Alec Tulev's shoulder.

Alec beamed.

"For later on then, brother," Jeff said and the four of us dispersed, Alec yelling back at us as we spilled away:

"OH! THANK YOU! THANK YOU, SIRS!"

The marble-walled ninth floor of City Hall was *alive* at 3:00 P.M. on a Friday, heaps of nervous humans decorated in a range of formalities: teams of young people in tuxes and bridesmaids' dresses sitting bob-legged on long, wooden benches next to older, quieter couples in jeans and T-shirts. Some wore sweaters, some shorts, some top hats and canes. Some wore long trains and veils, some pantsuits or maternity wear. Everyone was carrying cameras and posing or getting triplicate forms stamped by monotone-voiced clerks who seemed perfectly ruined on the whole swarm. Loren wore a bell-shaped white sleeveless dress. She smelled almost confectionary, her dark hair down, and she reacted to seeing me by first smiling then quickly dabbing sweat beads from my brow with a tissue. Loren's black-dressed mother was hovering, snapping photos at an alarming rate. Fay from LA trailed in an orange floral dress, Jeff Stibner in Loren's brother's suit (gray), Loren's brother in his own suit (blue), and his girlfriend in a loose golden sundress. My father, looking shockingly undiminished, was suited up in dark green, my thin brother uncomfortable and David Byrne–like in one of my father's hand-me-down ensembles. My mother wore a bright aquamarine blazer and a matching skirt—troubling leg scar also in attendance—and when the clerk needed a witness, Loren and I asked that her initials and signatures please verify our union.

My mother seemed to enjoy that; she hupped to order proudly.

Loren and I braced everyone for a bureaucratic stall, but almost instantly a robed justice, a sly-seeming woman who peered over her bifocals, beckoned our crew into her chamber, placed us around the room—Loren and me in the center—then presented us with a choice: "short version" or "long version."

"How long is the short version?" I asked.

"One minute."

"How long is the long version?" Loren asked.

"Three minutes."

One long version later we were all in an elevator, lowering downwards. Of the many sublime silences that weekend, this one remains my favorite. The elevators in City Hall had tall, spacious cars: majestic, bronze-hued and decorative, and no fewer than four other newly married couples rode down with our party to street level. Some were our age, but most were older or had clearly differing agendas for their union. But we were all bound by the same prickly, quiet wattage: one collective held breath. We moved slowly. I gripped Loren's warm hand. She leaned into my shoulder, the entire car mute and shifty as the floors chimed down, almost near burst, until a weary, thirties-looking woman—holding only the fingers on the veiny hand of a much older, much rougher-looking man with a patchy white goatee—said flatly before the doors split open to cough us out into the day:

"Alright folks. Where's the bar."

So many of my memories of that weekend's details have become unreliable, conflated with the photos of them in some post facto way. (For years I told the story of Alec Tulev as though it happened en route to a noon ceremony until Loren, only very recently, stopped me and said: "You know we got married in the late afternoon, right?") In the post-wedding photos I appear flush, red-cheeked and calm; pale, puffy, and dazed at the dinner after. I'm even more ghostlike and swollen in photos of Shawn Chipp's party the next night: out-of-town friends poured in, Jeff Stibner finally found coke for his nose, and I spent a large portion of the evening laying alone on a bed—my skin twitching, thundering heartbeat, yet so heavy-lidded and bone-tired—praying emptily for a nap.

Following the ceremony, Ethan had agreed to meet us for photos at Battery Park, a location we chose because of its closeness to City Hall and its riverside view. Ethan began snapping shots, first of Loren, then of Loren with her family. The only member of my own family present then was my brother, who stood alongside me as we watched our mother in the distance—again, arm wrapped around my father—shuffle and smoke.

My parents had cabbed as far as the streets would allow, but there was still a grand patch of park lawn between where the street ended and the riverfront began. My mother seemed, at least from where we stood, at odds with her immobility yet still somehow pleased with the leisure it provided her. During her breaks, which were many—the distance was at least four times that of last night's tiny, two-block-long plaza—she bent down, examined the bloom of a flower bed, or cast her gaze toward the boats on the Hudson River break, across to the Jersey City skyline. In no time Ethan had shot everyone, had even pulled Loren and me together for some couple photos, including a from-below shot of our newly ringed fists punching outwards, which failed to turn out as superhero-like as we'd hoped. Out of the corner of my eye, my mother still trailed. Jeff Stibner had at some point purchased a small bottle of whiskey. My brother—like me, no stranger to shadowy coping strategies— threw up his hands and joined Jeff and Loren's brother, pulling quietly from the bottle as we waited.

Not me. I was too busy seething.

I seem to return to this moment most when I think of that weekend, because it was the point at which I finally understood with an awful clarity why people had grown so impatient with me at Mark McKiernan's Ohio wedding two summers before; why they hissed when I couldn't accomplish something as simple as exiting a car.

You inherit a new, small universe with every catastrophe. But when the catastrophe is illness, it's your universe to steward, and it's already half-complete by the time you get it. Diagnoses, complications, final outcomes—those are rarely yours to fully mold. So you're appointed your illness's middle manager, its parking lot attendant, responsible for arranging people properly in its orbit. At Mark's wedding people bucked because they did not want to be arranged by a pale replacement groomsman and his specious hormone disfluency. They knew—and Loren knew—that I wasn't there out of bravery or selflessness or any other of the live-strong platitudes and clichés I'd later offer up. Whether I realized it or not, my illness and I had encroached on that experience only to prove it was possible.

And here we were again, my illness and I, on the same kind of sunlit day: Loren's mother checking her phone, a trio of suited men on a park bench swigging Crown Royal, Loren and the women ducked under the shade of tree branches, and Ethan shutter-clicking photos of us all locked in our distant politeness. We were positioned precisely where my mother and her illness had put us: watching without comment as my father escorted her unmended body patiently forward.

I suspect, as she made her slow way across that lawn, that my mother still truly believed in her own valiance, in the virtue of courage in place of good sense. It had been a difficult few years, and she was fed up with being sick, so she was driving hard through it like one might a wall. There was fractured nobility in the attempt. But it was my mother's absence of awareness—her inability, after so long, to *see* us—that I'd run out of ways to be patient with. My father, brother, and I had swarmed to her side for every fold in the saga of her sputtering heart, jammed our useless hands in our pockets and had our own hearts broken, only to steel ourselves months later to endure another brutal replay. I was so used to swelling with anger and frustration because my mother refused to get better. That afternoon I was angry because she refused to *be sick* better; to understand, or at least acknowledge, the audience of her pageantry and the nature of our pained, conflicted devotion to it. I wanted her to grasp the shape of the universe that her illness had given her and finally, *please*, place us in it accordingly.

The photos that day were cursory. My mother, my brother, my father, and I stood inches apart, not touching. I didn't say anything mean or dismissive to my mother, or to my father, her frustrated accomplice. *Just smile and pose, then on to the next thing*, I thought, while underneath my skin something rotten moved in my blood, buckling, looking for a way to break.

At the party the trivia writers threw for us that night, I sat on a couch numb-handed. People served me drinks, and I drank them. Fay from LA had brought her friends, and Jeff Stibner and my brother tried desperately to sleep with each of them until the bartender—who caught a glimpse of my brother's face, looking every bit like the underager he was—banished them back to my apartment. The trivia writers all trickled in with their blazers and their movie quotes; my day-job coworkers sat huddled at one table for their obligatory hour. Loren floated between them all, a skilled conversationalist as always, taking compliments, making well-timed jokes. I sat toward the back of the bar immersed in a nameless fog. I'd taken more cortisol, 25 mg now, but whatever was happening with my hormones had worsened. Things moved too darkly or too quickly. I was gripped by an odd conversational paralysis. Words I wanted to say, I couldn't—at least not with the speed or intonations I was accustomed to—so I smiled and spat out banalities and thank you's in my new suit and red tie.

I don't remember who I was talking to—that night seems now an amalgam of noisy faces—likely one of the trivia writers. Maybe Akil the Rabid Steelers Fan, or Patricia the Former Editor of Several Books I Loved, or Todd Who Talked Sadly about Drinking a Case of Beer in One Sitting, or Rick of the Perpetually Near-Financed Indy Film, or Jared Who Rick Once Cruelly Locked in the Men's Bathroom. Whoever it was, as they went on I glimpsed in my periphery the white of Loren's dress. I reached my hand up, ran my numb fingers across the material on Loren's dress back, slid them lightly and thankfully across its surface for a long, tender span of seconds, until whomever I was talking with stopped abruptly and asked something like:

"Having fun there, buddy?"

I looked to my right. It wasn't Loren next to me. It was Ethan. And the material I was caressing so lovingly was not the back of Loren's dress. It was Ethan's white oxford.

The next day, after I gave Jeff Stibner sixty dollars of my trivia-writing money to cab to Newark, after Loren's mother and brother took their kind leave and my parents and brother made the turn onto the Brooklyn-Queens Expressway, Loren and I turned all the lights off in our apartment and shut the blinds. It was midafternoon now. Our heads were on cold pillows, ringed hands folded into one another, my arms and chest still weak and twitchy, wrung out, her slow breath in my ear. We collapsed into each other's bodies like flattened boxes. And then my body and its fake hormones slept for sixteen hours.

PART FIVE

CH. 19

JEWELRY

Skuh-*leez*-ay, yes?"

Dr. Anatoli was peering down at the name on my patient file, trying through his accent—which broke true Italian, though from what region I couldn't tell—to determine the manner in which I had chosen to use my name. His voice was low and slow like a door creak. "Skuh-*leez*-ay," he said again, looking to me as if to say, *This is how we say it where I, and you (I presume), come from.*

"For one side of my family, yes," I said. "Our side pronounces it Skuh-*leece*. We don't talk much to the Skuh-*leez*-ays. It's a whole thing. Warring factions."

His assistant, a rotund, blond man in a canary bow tie, sat in a chair at the corner of the exam room, taking notes like all the other assistants I'd seen: nervously, obediently, frantically.

"Okay, small difference, good name," Dr. Anatoli said, then looked up at me, glasses loose on his nose bridge, and surveyed my person. The exam room was nondescript and thin, with a top-of-the-line desktop computer whose monitor was keyed to a very intimidating-looking database. Anatoli was in a chair next to it, clicking checkboxes and typing information as I gave it to him. Even after three-plus years in rooms like this, I still sat nervous at the end of his exam table, wanting to impress him, legs dangling like a child's.

"Your belly is very large," he said. "We shall reduce your cortisol."

He nodded and hummed. I told him I was a little tired, hadn't been sleeping well.

"Sexual function is good?" he asked.

"A-OK," I said.

"'Like bull,'" I said, with air quotes.

I looked to the bow-tied assistant in the corner, who cracked a smile. But Dr. Anatoli didn't. He flipped through pages of notes, three years' worth of hormonal profile.

"I keep waiting for the other shoe to drop," I told him. "Three years now, still good in that 'arena.'" Again with the air quotes.

And it was true. Aside from the No T Experiment there had been no loss of function or libido, and by now I was equal parts curious and paranoid as to why, waiting for the absence to come, hoping Anatoli, with his objective eye, might be able to tell me when. But he did not look up. His eyes peered through the bifocals into my file, my pages, shaking his head, nodding. Then he said flatly, with still no eye contact:

"Eet ees your Italian blood."

It was late summer, 2005. Place: Baltimore, Maryland, in a highly regarded endocrine facility in the outpatient building of a hulking hospital complex an hour's train ride from Washington, DC. Loren and I had moved to DC a few weeks earlier, for her to take a job at a K Street nonprofit, and for me to begin graduate school across the Potomac in Virginia, at the only place that would have me: a small, well-staffed creative writing program shoehorned into what my program's director called a "transitioning commuter school" in a moneyed suburb at the tip of the DC Metro line. The campus looked, on its most striking, sun-fueled days, like a bookish mini-mall.

It was a change, but not a flip one. I'd learned over the last year that my excitement for writing software manuals had a limit. And for two years I'd been a part of a quorum of late night trivia writers, several of whom had now launched off to stunning new destinations: gigs as quip-making pundits on VH1 shows like *I Love the '70s/'80s/'90s*, staff on spoof news websites, story editors for comic books like *Hawkman*, or news bloggers for *ESPN*, *The Sporting News*, *Entertainment Weekly*. The longer I stayed, the more the place proved itself a holding pen for those with truer callings. The people who left became mythic immediately upon their upward departures. When the pilot for a show called *Crossballs* aired on Comedy Central—a *Daily Show*–like parody of CNN's *Crossfire*, written by two guys who'd been, just months before, our sad, cranky coworkers—we trivia writers stopped work and hunched around a single TV giddy with hope.

Soon enough, I was eager for my own graduation. I'd seen in the year since my wedding that aspiration could be a simple, practical thing, and grew increasingly impatient with mini-features on in-ear headphones and celebrity pet culture. Even watching television for money, something I thought I'd never tire of, something I thought would take a spoiled idiot to dislike, became not enough. I called off shifts more than I showed up for them, and when I did, I pissed around. Frank the Recent Fiction MFA Grad and I tried our best to slip vulgar information into the trivia questions to see if someone, anyone (our editors, or the game-players, who I'm still convinced never existed) would ever really notice:

What did Gob Bluth do when Buster Bluth refused to "stand up to the man" at the construction site?
A. Danced like a chicken (correct)
B. Called him a traitor
C. Said he was weak-willed
D. Executed a hobo, gangland-style

It went on like that for months. I felt like what I wrote: trivia. Stagnant, benign, impactless. I wanted, I told people, to "move in a more literary direction," and "have more time for my own work." I had little sense what that work would even be, but I felt defiant, chin raised. I'd run out of use for it, I told people, and when I was admitted to the program just outside of DC, right where Loren's new job was, I wove happily through the office(s) of my job(s) like I'd just been appointed the prince of a newer, more useful nation.

Then there was the matter of breaking up with Dr. Walla, which I mentally rehearsed for weeks. We'd had our frustrations: I was not the best patient, and there was still part of me that wondered whether she was more interested in treating the person or the statistic. But her coverage was the only coverage I knew, and I was scared to move on from it. We'd forged something unique, I thought. It's not rare, I realize, to project a false value onto your doctor-patient arrangement, to believe that your convalescent arc somehow bonds itself to theirs as a caretaker, that both parties are evenly enriched by the pairing. The fantasy was lame, predictable, and I knew it but felt it anyway. When I broke the news at the beginning of the summer, two months before we moved, it happened something like this:

ME: "We're moving to Washington, DC, at the end of the summer."

HER: "Email Dr. Sam Anatoli. He's the top pituitary specialist at the top endocrine department at the top hospital in the area, which also might be the top hospital and research facility in the entire United States. Here's his info. Take care."

And that was it.

No hug, no quiet moment of shared confidence. No *We have done good work against the forces of hormonal anomalies.* Just a cold piercing of a fatty slab of my ass (left cheek that month), then off to the A train. See you at the end of the summer, then never again.

Weeks later, Dr. Anatoli, after a very cursory once-over, said he saw something in my most recent blood tests that hinted toward progress.

Possible onset of the Gamma Knife radiation, he said.

He then reversed or reduced every prescription Dr. Walla had given me, striking them down with his cutting accent, which I'd decided was Neapolitan—later my family loved this turn of events, treated by a true, real-life Dago—his plump assistant scribbling new dosages as fast as his boss gave them, handing me small slips of paper to take with me to my new pharmacy in DC.

The blood tests and MRI films he'd seen weren't new. They were the same films and readings that Dr. Walla had been look-ing at for months, but he ordered me another, newer round of bloodwork and procedures, and then—suspecting that my tumor was gone, that the radiation had at last made it to the loitering bit of tumor on my carotid—he cut me from the Sandostatin shots for the first time in thirty months.

There was one thing he and Dr. Walla agreed on whole-heartedly.

"No MedicAlert bracelet on your wrist, I see."

"I know, I *know*," I said.

"Mister Skuh-*leez*-ay, that ees no good," he said. "No good. You must."

He motioned to his assistant, who shuffled through his folder for a pamphlet, the same pamphlet Dr. Walla had given me a year before, the same pamphlet that sat crumpled and torn at the bottom of my now-tattered shoulder bag. And like Dr.

Walla had, Anatoli's assistant quickly scribbled on it ADRENAL INSUFFICIENCY, STEROIDS, then handed it over like he was issuing a parking violation.

"Okay, I get it," I said, smiling.

"You must," Anatoli said, not smiling at all.

My new primary care physician felt the same way, just differently. She was one of a slur of names listed as "preferred providers" by Loren's anemic, nonprofit-sanctioned health plan. Where my old GP was gruff and disinterested—or I seemed to remember him that way, I hadn't seen the man in over three years—my new one was young, abundantly pregnant and, like my initial crew of young neurosurgeons three years before, indulged in certain forms of congeniality while she pecked my information onto a laptop screen with a high-tech plastic pen.

"Oh, don't get the bracelet, dude," she said. "Go for the *dog tags.*"

But there were, I found, more than just dog tags. The medical ID racket was a robust one, with MedicAlert leading the pack. The Internet was littered with retailers, both wholesale and independent, pushing all kinds of custom jewelry aimed at all manner of sick people and their non-sick lifestyles: children, "active" and "elegant" sick people, sick people who wished to "stay safe and in style." (In recent years the market has grown to include even the "bolder" jewelry of Rockstar ID—"Medical IDs That Rock!"—featuring thick leather bracelets adorned in studs, silver chains, zippers, and metal skulls.)

Still: none of it appealed, or fit, or felt—despite some very contrary evidence—all that necessary. Loren seemed just as put off by the idea, which only validated my own hesitation, even if our instincts didn't hold as much water as they once had. We'd reluctantly backed into marriage only to find that it was a shockingly welcome fit. We'd been together for nearly eight years at the time of our wedding, and expected it to be a mere formality, that things would stay unaltered. But we spent the weeks after in a state of giggly, bewildered irony.

"Hello there, *wife*," I would say when I came home.

"Greetings, *husband*," and so on.

Then those words crept more readily and lovingly into our conversations, and I began to detect a heightened respect from people when I used them. If, for instance, I said I was "going home to the girlfriend" to avoid a late night with the trivia writers, it triggered an inane discussion of whether or not I was "whipped." Insert the words *my wife* into that same statement and their eyes gleamed with obedient understanding. "*You're* married?" an older, single female co-editor at the children's publisher once gasped after glancing at my band during a meeting. People took us more seriously, so we took *ourselves* more seriously, and grew attached to the few bits of accouterment our wedding had provided. Loren and I had both endured episodes in which we'd briefly misplaced our wedding rings, and were surprised at how anxious and frantic those episodes turned us; how quickly we'd come to see the rings as essential artifacts of a more seismic shift that we couldn't yet voice, even as we reveled in it.

We didn't see the same potential in medical ID jewelry. Now in its third year, my illness had become *our* illness, had matured into a thing we'd both learned to contend with as a unit. Wedding weekend aside, there had been no further breakdowns since—or ones that, at least, I didn't fend off quickly with a bump of cortisol, a tweak in the AndroGel. I harbored my own private worries about the tumor's possible return, but as a relationship obstacle we'd proudly relocated my illness to our ever-growing list of Things We Knew How to Handle.

"Did you take your meds, *husband*?" Loren would say after my mother would call late, wine-soaked and forlorn, to hem and haw about procedures past, or her feelings about my own procedures past, or sometimes nothing at all, quiet for long spans on the end of the line.

"Excellent call, *wife*," I'd say.

But the medical ID jewelry didn't fit the dynamic we'd worked so hard to cull together. It seemed, even at its most "stylish," grossly unindicative: too impersonal and homogenous. It wasn't *us*.

"What about if you put your dosages on a little sheet in your wallet?" Loren asked one day.

"How many doctors will think to look there?" I said. "And I lose my wallet what—twice a month?"

I had, in fact, left my wallet in a cab that week.

"I could get a tattoo," I said a few days later, "that just reads I HAVE NO PITUITARY GLAND. On my wrist. Or on my leg?"

"You could do that," Loren said, "but then you'd be an asshole."

It continued like that for a long time.

CH. 28

YACHT PEOPLE

Shortly after the DC move, with the summer weather still hovering stubborn in the new fall air, my father called me late on a Thursday to ask a favor.

"Your mother and I are thinking of coming down this weekend," he said. "We want to take a look at some yachts."

"*Yachts?*" I said.

"I figure we can all take a drive out to the docks under the bay bridge," my father said. The Chesapeake Bay was forty minutes outside DC, beneath which was a series of interconnected dock houses, crab shacks and marinas. "There's one there with a few models your mother and I are interested in."

"How so?"

"We have a couple models dog-eared," he said.

He kept saying that. *Models.*

"What, like to *buy*?" I asked.

My father said yes.

In recent months, he had been stalking a new career, secretly, telling only my mother and me. Clients he'd worked with over the last three decades, people in all parts of the country, had made certain overtures, he said. Places wanted him, or had hinted so. And they were far more corporate venues, bigger and more known than my family's regional business. With my brother about to graduate college, my father and mother wanted, he told me, a more solitary life than they had in Pittsburgh, something far less entangled, where he and my mother could exist apart from attachments or beholdenness.

But more than anything, my father said, he wanted more money. He was tired of being undervalued. So he'd asked for my help building a résumé—something that, as a lifelong employee of a company whose chairman of the board taught him to drive a car, he'd never had to do. I had by then become a résumé artist, compulsive about seeking, getting, then juggling as many jobs as the day allowed. Within weeks of arriving in DC I was a stringer for two regional magazines, tutoring undergrads, and editing case reviews for a law professor, all while picking up contract gigs at the children's publisher in New York and taking a full class load—it was the only way I knew how to do higher education. So I was excited to help with anything that would allow my father the breakaway he seemed to crave, the one he and my mother had worked so hard to give me.

My father appeared far more serious about the idea than he ever had. During those long, marathon talks we'd had while my mother was in the operating room, my father often made curt hints at defection from the business—"Maybe I'll just head to ____ "—but they always seemed like tales he'd told himself about his own worth to will forth a sense of vigor. Now my father and I had long, brass-tacks phone calls regarding his "goals," what he hoped to accomplish with the move, wherever it would be, what he could "bring to the table," and his staggered evolution within his family's company: from estimator, to VP, to defector, back down to midmanager, then back up to VP again.

We talked most candidly, most surprisingly, about his salary. I'd never thought it was a heaping sum. We lived worriless, but not well. We ate Sam's Club frozen chimichangas by the case. We drove used Hondas and Fords until they died. My brother's clothes had once been my clothes. Still, given the holidays at my grandfather's expansive vacation homes, one in Indian Lake, another in Fort Lauderdale, and the family meals at country clubs (of which his father and brother, the company's current president, were members), I'd assumed my parents lived more than a scrounging, barren existence.

But over the course of our conversations I learned his take-home, by far the highest it had ever been—he'd recently asked for a raise, which his little brother begrudgingly granted him—was still barely enough to maintain a home, let alone send two children through college, especially now that my mother was a doctor-ordered, fifty-three-year-old retiree with zero pension. My father's salary was only slightly higher than Loren's, which meant that as a vice president of a sixty-year-old commercial heating and air-conditioning firm—one whose logo was slapped onto fleets of white Silverados and F-10s that couriered sheet metal and heating coils to job sites in Pittsburgh, West Virginia, Ohio, New York, Virginia, Maryland, Kentucky—he made less per year than the combined efforts of a pair of twenty-seven-year-olds in a one-bedroom apartment, one a low-level child welfare policy analyst and the other a grad student on a stipend.

All of this is to say that my parents were not yacht people and had never been yacht people, which at least explained the second half of my father's favor request for the weekend, a two-day period over which he and my mother and I would dock hop in search of 42-foot vessels fit enough to bravely navigate the great waterways of our country's eastern coastline:

"So," my father asked me, "can we sleep on your futon?"

That Saturday afternoon we were in thick, sun-warmed air, weaving through the green, branch-shaded back roads of the Chesapeake basin, listening to *The Best of Van Morrison*, one of the five CDs my parents ever listened to, which skipped ugly over the second verse of "Moondance." My mother sat in the front seat with a map of North Carolina's inlet shore towns, showing me the ones she'd circled as potential destinations, places where she and my father and their imaginary boat would reactivate their lives.

"We want to get a small little house here, in this town," my mother said. She tapped the spot on the map. "It's right by the water, no frills, just one bedroom and a dock for the boat. That's all I want. We'll mostly be out on the water," she went on.

I agreed from the back seat. It all sounded great, I told her, and I don't know if I meant it or if I didn't. She flipped the page, moved on to the next town, said the same thing. She had identified a series of pre-fabrications, rubber-stamped boho dock towns all offering the same kind of easiness, the same loosened life type.

It wasn't something I was prepared for, but I should have been. My parents' unfolding plan was, in small ways, reminiscent of the ill-fated move to New Mexico when I was in middle school. But that plan never lived beyond its own canned grandeur, past the cheap wall frame paintings of sunset mesas my mother had hung all over our living room. This plan, the yacht plan, carried a surprising level of detail and practicality. They'd hatched Plan As, Plan Bs, and Plan Cs. And yet, aside from short jaunts on my grandfather's pontoon at the lake house, my parents had never hinted at a nautical inclination, let alone a simmering desire to remake their lives around a 42-foot boat.

But that didn't mean I wasn't happy to hear it. My mother had healed moderately well in the last year from her bypasses and stents. She was walking nightly around her neighborhood, by herself now, exercising, using her free time to unbind from stress. She'd warmed to my marriage to Loren in a way neither of us had expected her to. She'd begun calling Loren her "daughter." "And how's my daughter doing," she'd say when she called. Aside from the occasional dip back into self-pity—I still never picked

up the phone after 9:00 P.M.—it was all silent on the heart problem front. No reports from doctors regarding her decline.

My mother lit a cigarette, blew the smoke out the car window.

"I just want to be away," she said. "I like it down in North
Carolina."

"Have you guys gone there recently?" I asked.

"Nope, never been there," she said. "But I like it."

My father wanted to know about fuel efficiency, about engine speed. He held his hands on his hips. He was concerned
about "hull space." The salesman was scarecrow tall with a red
shirt and a gray-blond beard, wiry, Adam's apple, with hair curls
springing out from his sleeveless shoulders, and he knew how
to answer my father's questions in a way that made the man
feel like he was being taken seriously. The salesman presented
options, told my father there were models that might fit what
he was looking for, but if not, they might be at another dock
a few miles down the road. My father acted as though he already knew where those places were and was well versed in
what they had to offer. The salesman and my father went back
and forth like this, neither seeming sincere: my father nodding
his head, palm on his beard, the salesman saying things like
"Oh, you *definitely* want that." It was as though each person was
poorly reenacting a sale they'd once watched happen, though
not the same sale.

"How serious is this?" I asked my mother. I stood next to
her on the dock. It was late in the afternoon now, a steady
wind, my bare arms tight from the chill.

"What do you mean?" my mother asked me.

My father and the salesman had opened the doors to the engine hull, were kneeling to the floor of the boat deck, looking down into the engine, discussing the boat's guts.

"Does this mean Dad got a new gig?"

"No, that was never—" My mother laughed and waved her hand, like she was pushing something away.

"Good year at work then?" I asked her.

The price on this particular boat was over two hundred thousand dollars. My father thanked the salesman, closed the engine hull, shook his hand, said he'd be back in touch later, once he saw those other models, at that other dock, sometime soon. I kept on with the questions to my mother—"Do you guys have a time frame? Is Dad going to retire? You guys are only in your early fifties, how's that even going to *work*—"

"You know," my mother finally said, "sometimes it's good to have dreams, ok?"

On the way back toward the highway, my father made a quick turn onto a dirt road that wove through thin, tall trees with large houses plotted among them.

"Making a stop," he said. He was excited, spitting out a whistle as "Domino" played on the stereo. We pulled into the driveway of a modest home on the shoreline, brown brick and a one-car garage on top of a hillside that led down to a small, personal dock. A white, weathered boat clunked against the steel lip of the dock wall. My mother recognized the place moments before we arrived.

"Jim and Joan's, *Jim and Joan's*," she said.

I remembered Jim and Joan from when I was younger. After a period of post-childbirth friendlessness, Jim and Joan, a married couple that my parents knew from high school, reemerged in their lives. They didn't have kids, and reintroduced my parents to things they hadn't done since before my brother and I were alive. The four of them flocked eagerly toward the Civic Arena for the Pittsburgh leg of Genesis's Invisible Touch Tour in '87, after which Jim and Joan were at my house every weekend for Steelers games or to play board games and, I discovered much later, to duck into the basement to smoke pot out of the black porcelain bowl my parents kept from their teen years. And then, one day, Jim and Joan were gone again.

The two couples reunited years later, when I was in high school. Jim and Joan were still childless, but now they had a boat stationed in southern Maryland. My parents would pack my brother into the back of the Ford, then spend weekends getting deep neck tans and crabbing on the Chesapeake—which was, of course, my cue to call Jeff Stibner and beckon all the beer, Mad Dog 20/20 and gravity bongs we could fit into my parents' home, after which all the people we liked soon arrived. But that had been ten years ago. With my brother nearly done with college—two years in Indiana on a soccer scholarship, then a transfer back to Pittsburgh, just like me—my mother told me they'd reconnected with Jim and Joan again, had been ducking down to the Chesapeake basin even before Loren and I moved into the vicinity, crabbing and drinking beer again, anchoring out overnight, listening over the lapping waves to Jim

talking about his new life as a pension-funded federal government retiree, to Joan talking about hers as an early-retired
heath care worker.

My father left the keys in the ignition, grabbed the info packet
the boat salesman had handed him before we left the dock, the
one featuring a few models that might be what the salesman
called "your size," and jogged up to Jim and Joan's front door.
He knocked. He went to the back door, knocked. Basement
door: no luck there either, so my father came back to the car
and rested his forearms on the driver's-side open window.

"Should we wait?" he asked.

"What are you doing," my mother said.

"I want to show Jim and Joan."

"We should go," she said.

"They might be at the store or something."

"And if they're not? I'm not going to sit in their driveway
and wait," my mother said. "Someone will think we're staking
the goddamn house out."

It went on like this for several minutes, my mother morti-
fied, my father elated, me in the back seat, a little sunk-
en-hearted for them both. My father grabbed a Sharpie from
the console, slapped the yacht packet onto the hood of the
SUV as it idled, then sketched out what looked like a long
note. I couldn't read it, but I could tell he was writing big, in
caps, underlining the words. He took the packet to the front
porch and slid it in behind the screen door, resting it against
the main door like a presentation. Then we were back on the

highway, "Moondance" skipping on the stereo again, the three of us moving steady against a falling sun back toward Washington, DC, so that my parents could change clothes, settle in, and rest their big, dreaming heads on my flat, shitty futon.

CH. 21

A HISTORY IN CARICATURE

There was a midsized dog named Mike at the party, and before I realized that I spent the first minutes there wondering if someone I didn't know in some other room was talking to me or about me. *There's Mike*, I heard. *Oh, I love Mike! Where's he going? Can Mike eat that? Sit, Mike. Sit.* I was at the Northern Virginia home of a married pair of faculty poets at my new graduate program, for a celebration to honor my incoming class, or at least the idea of us: budding poets and fictionists and journalists. I'd come with Kara, a dry, hilarious short story writer, and Ben, a bearded poet who minutes earlier had sold his rusted-over Volvo to someone he'd found online—right in front of the house where the party was, as though he did this kind of thing all the time—then pocketed hundreds of dollars from the sale as we entered the party together, bound by a pact of newness. We were co-workers of a sort: part-time tutors in our university's writing center. Early on, this was one of the few ways we understood how to refer to ourselves in grad school, which was proving a curious exercise in compartmentalized identity. "What genre?" was the most common lead-off we encountered from upperclassmen and other first-years, and our answers served as social anchors to awkward talks about books and hopes that felt like miniature tests of intellect and prowess that neither party knew how to pass yet. (Loren, the child welfare policy analyst, decided right away to keep her presence scarce at parties. "If I go to another one of these," she said, "I'm wearing a button on my shirt that says NO GENRE.")

For me the idea of a compartmentalized identity had become something more convoluted than tutor, or genre representative, or Human Mike at a Dog Mike party. A week before the first-year celebration I'd walked home from a late tutoring session at a satellite campus near my apartment—windy and warm along the sidewalk, my shoulder bag heavy with books—and received a phone call from Dr. Anatoli.

"Skuh-*leez*-ay, I have had a look and see at your most recent tests and the Gamma Knife radiation," he said. "I think it has taken full effect."

I was, it seemed then, the only person on the sidewalk for blocks.

"It's gone?" I asked. "Completely?"

"Yes, yes. I think it has been gone for quite some time, yes," Anatoli said.

Like in the early days of my diagnosis, everything seemed too new or had changed too swiftly to understand how to feel about the news. Yes, yes: radiation setting in was a definitive end to one medical threat. And unless my case was far more rare than we'd already assumed, the brain tumor wouldn't return, which marked the beginning of—what, exactly? I still thought of the tumor as my life's prime disaster far more than the murky damage it had done. If this news from Anatoli *was* a true sea change, maybe embrace it, I thought. Get a new avatar. I certainly had my pick of them. But which one fit? What, if not illness, might I be made of now?

I started by talking about New York City at the first-year party. I said nothing interesting about it. I said nothing interesting about New York City in a kitchen while eating wings off a small plate. I said nothing interesting about New York City while on the deck with a beer in my hand, while petting Mike the Dog, while talking to a confessional poet who'd said she had spent the last weekend on acid with musicians, eating cherries out of a bowl in a Dupont Circle efficiency.

And I said nothing interesting about New York City while bumming an additive-free cigarette from a sad-eyed poet at the fire pit in the backyard, where I ended up for most of the party. The poet had graduated the year before. He spoke slowly. He was earnest. He said this party was "the best part of every year," then heralded the faculty ("The quality . . . of specialists . . . in truly language-driven poetry . . . is exceptional here, I think . . ."). He seemed sad to no longer be a student. His eyes portrayed a fresh and frustrated aimlessness. He wanted, it was clear, to be back in the context he'd known so well, taking classes, having opinions.

The talk veered toward his little cousin, a ten-year-old who liked to write. The poet said he'd been working with his cousin on the weekends, walking him through basic poetic forms, talking with him about diction and pace. He liked working with kids, he said, and might want to do that now, for his life. He talked about how rewarding it was to see progress in his ten-year-old cousin, how much he valued the "small victories," as he called them. I nodded obediently. It was hard to follow the rhythm and thrust of his conversation, but he seemed so adamant about this relationship with poetry and his cousin that I felt almost like I was consoling him.

"Its just . . . so hard with him sometimes," he said. He was looking down at his beer now, staring into it. "His cognitive skills are shit . . . he's got this . . . really rare brain tumor."

Goddammit, I thought. *Of course he does.*

The first public acromegalic might not have been a person at all. It might, instead, have been a puppet. Researchers have theorized that Mr. Punch of Punch and Judy fame, the storied, often comically violent Italian hand puppet featured in street shows dating back to the Roman Empire, was made by some unknown Geppetto precisely in an acromegalic's image: thick neck, distended gut, hunchbacked, big-nosed, with what one report called "prominent facial features and large hands." Even Dr. Leonard Mark, author of that first-ever memoir of acromegaly, floated the theory that Punch's tendency to hit Judy and their puppet child during shows (it was, I suppose, a simpler time under Caesar's reign) was driven by headaches caused by the pressure of a pituitary tumor.

"The history of Mr. Punch," one researcher said in 2006, "is the history of caricature." Caricature runs through the narratives of some of the most famous public giants and acromegalics in history. Rondo Hatton, brute of the '50s horror films, never found work outside of what his image granted him. Each year the Rondo Hatton Awards, which "celebrate the best in classic horror research," are awarded to trailblazing horror filmmakers. The winners receive a bust of Hatton's large, deep-valleyed, acromegalic head, his expression—taken, I imagine, from a still of him as The Creeper—frozen at its most ghastly.

The acting career of Eddie Carmel, Diane Arbus's "Jewish Giant," failed just as Rondo Hatton's did. His small roles led nowhere; his audio recordings remained largely unheard. He died at age thirty-six, never able to eclipse the image Arbus captured two years prior. "You know how every mother has that nightmare when she's pregnant that her baby will be born a monster?" Arbus told *The New Yorker* while she was shooting Carmel in the sixties. "I think I got that in the mother's face as she glares up at Eddie, thinking 'OH MY GOD, NO!'"

Shepard Fairey, reflecting on his decision to launch his OBEY campaign in the late eighties, which still reigns as some of the world's most prominent street art imagery to date, nearly twenty five years after André René Roussimoff's death from heart failure: "He is so ugly! It is brilliant!"

For three years now I'd preached an incessant gospel of freak illness, built with hypotheses and waiting rooms, needles and experiments; big moments where I felt nothing, and tiny moments where I felt so much so fast that my body's motor seemed to stop itself cold. In my mind I was shoving forward the parts of my pituitary tumor's tale that made me special, the parts that made me unlike everyone else. I wanted to replace whatever meaning I feared people projected onto me when they saw my face, my eyes, my hands. "Your feet look so *weird,*" my brother-in-law once said to me, clueless; I once watched a female friend actually *wince and gag* when someone mistook us for a couple.

Talking about my tumor, being so open, almost forceful about it, was a matter of getting ahead of the story. It was PR. I spun. But what if, just like Rondo and Eddie and Andre, going that public only accidentally emboldened a caricature of me? What if, after all that bluster, I was merely making myself into a puppet for my own illness?

The sad-eyed poet's story about his cousin, at one point in the recent past, would have been what my mother might call "easy pickings." *Solidarity for the Brotherhood of the Rare Brain Tumor,* I might have said. Now I wasn't so sure. I hesitated as he talked more. I found myself passive and pitying. *Oh no. That's horrible.* It was a frustrating place to be. I wanted it gone.

But I only knew one way to make that happen.

"I had a rare brain tumor too," I said.

Something different happened when I told the rest. The beats felt off. The rhythm lagged. Jokes felt forced and alien.

A reversal happened, and not the good kind: the poet offered back the very look of intent and uncomfortable concern that this story was meant to demolish. I felt stranded in my own tale, unsure of how to move through it. He seemed to want *something else* from me, and I found myself talking about the parts I had never talked about, the frustrations with my body that I'd kept from everyone, even Loren. I talked about my distrust of my own eyes, and the eyes of those around me, how I felt betrayed by my own bloodstream.

It was not good party talk. I knew this as it was happening.

"What I'm trying to say," I told the poet, through some uplifting, busted logic, "is that good can come of those situations, you know? That brain tumors can be good things?"

That's what I said: *Brain tumors can be good things.*

"I don't think my little cousin would tell you there's anything good about his brain tumor, man," he said.

An anomaly, I thought as I rode home, Kara driving, Ben in front, me in the back. *A matter of audience*, I thought. *The rules still apply.* I'd been relying on them since 2002, though not in any formal way. They existed in my head, things I would tell myself when the opportunity materialized. *Undercut sympathy. Have bait.* When I came home from the party, I tried them out again, on a much grander scale. I wrote all the rules down: a tiny, ironic social manual for being sick in a healthy world. I wrote steps and sub-steps. I put the key phrases in bold. I offered tips. Then I brought all twenty-plus pages of them to my graduate writing workshop, a crew of nine people whose job it was to sit in a small room and learn how to talk seriously about learning how to write seriously.

"Here are the rules," I said to the workshop.

"Who are they for?" the workshop said back.

"Me," I said. "They're my rules."

"Yes, but if you already know them," the workshop said, "why are you writing them down?"

"For people to read," I said.

"Which people," said the workshop. "Like: now. Who are you writing these rules for *now*?"

PART SIX

CH. 22

PERHAPS NOTHING,
PERHAPS EVERYTHING

For the next seven years, I never got better. I just got boring.

So much of illness post-Gamma Knife, post-Sando-statin, was just that: day-to-day, livable illness at its most mundane, most uninteresting. I scheduled check-ins every six months with Dr. Anatoli through the scheduling office at the Baltimore hospital. Two weeks before each appointment, his office—he had a new endocrine fellow or assistant each time, as opposed to Errol, who seemed for Dr. Walla more of a long-term, Sonny Corleone–type—would mail me a lab sheet for a blood test. I'd take the lab sheet to a remote DC facility with a robotic name like LabTech or MedCorp, where I'd sit amongst the five or ten people there for either an employer- or court-ordered piss test, all of us wordless and slouched, spread around a gray, tiled waiting room not unlike what you might see at a car dealership or a Pep Boys. The only distraction we were granted was the drug-company-sponsored "media centre" in the corner of the room, playing its loop of sedate pharmaceutical infomercials on a tiny, dust-covered TV/VCR. I'd hear my name, walk through a dim hallway, and take a seat in a back room across from an unfascinated person in scrubs holding test tubes and a butterfly needle.

Two weeks later I'd take the train an hour up to Baltimore, to Dr. Anatoli's office on the seventh floor of the hospital's outpatient center, which featured two bunker-like outposts where I had to sign in with an official wearing a sweater. Many forms, many stamps. I had an orange card that held my patient records, and they ran it through a machine, after which I was directed toward another machine by the waiting area, where I pushed a button that corresponded with my doctor's last name. Like in a DMV or a supermarket deli, I took a number on a slip of paper that the machine spat out, then waited for forty-five minutes in one of the five separate waiting pens, staring at news racks loaded with pamphlets about caregiver retreats and dystonia. Next to me were always scores of other busted people with canes and scars, waiting their forty-five minutes, too, all of us glaring angrily at the lighted board above us reading, in slow intervals, NOW SERVING STATION 3.

At Dr. Walla's office it was always just me. There wasn't even a waiting room, only a door directly to her office, and I knocked on it. *Hey, Dr. Walla. Hey, Errol.* In and out in twenty-five minutes.

———

Absence has a system, too. The plight of my hormones, or lack of them, worked its way toward a dull predictability. I moved from ketchup packets of testosterone to the more popular, dick-looking pump. I bought a two-week pill divider for my chalky pills. Of the many gaps in my hormonal cache, the one that proved a repeat, serious danger was the same throughout. Stress—because of my inability to produce enough cortisol to endure it, or to have enough cortisol in my blood already to confront it when it came—had the potential to collapse my circulatory system (or worse).

Which means that I spent the next few years working on a fluid, personal, definition of the word *stress*: trying to determine its root, its shape, and what, exactly, it meant for me to have to work so hard to avoid it.

For instance:

2006, JANUARY, WASHINGTON, DC: The Pittsburgh Steelers are about to conquer the Indianapolis Colts in a divisional playoff game in the National Football League. Fourth quarter, just over one minute left. They're on the one-yard line and only need to ice the game with a touchdown for what would be, without question, a shockingly improbable win over a heavy Super Bowl favorite. I'm standing in front of the television, on the phone with a high school friend who still lives in Pittsburgh.

We're watching together, talking on our phones, saying things like *Fuck yeah* and *Yer goddamn right* with swift aggression because with this win the Steelers will, in moments, be better than the absolute best team in the NFL, which means that Pittsburgh, the place that spawned us, will also be, today, a far better place—if not to live, then to at least *be from*.

Loren's in between the kitchen and the bathroom and the bedroom, moving around, prepping laundry. I'm a foot from the TV, standing, saying *Holy fucking shit* loud into my phone when running back and certain Hall-of-Famer Jerome Bettis—who's about to throw his slow, fat body across the goal line for the touchdown we need—fumbles. It's a high-arching fumble that sends the Colts, ball in hand, back the other direction, running jaggedly, to steal the game. I've dropped my phone on the floor. I'm on my knees in front of the TV, screaming high-pitched from my gut in disbelief, as our quarterback—somehow, peddling back, weaving in the least graceful way imaginable—latches onto a Colt's ankle, halting the whole ruinous transaction. Feet from me I hear my friend's voice kazoo through my phone speaker.

My hands: sensationless. My chest, too. My heartbeat is a tightened metronome, a foreign, rapid glug. The Colts' place-kicker, the best in the league, lines up, kicks to send the game to overtime, a prospect I know I simply cannot handle. My hands are shaking, not in a nervous or dramatic fanboy way, but in a way that pulses hard through my forearms and somehow tightens my throat. I can't talk, or can barely. At once, I'm deeply tired. My center is numb and quivery as the Colts' ace kicker *misses* (holy shit), and the Steelers *still win* (holy shit), and I'm still on my knees, still in the living room. All I can say to Loren in the kitchen, the only words I can make my brain put together and call out are, "Baby—can you—bring me—my cortisol?" And even after that, the shaking, now a receded after-tremble, won't stop for more than two hours.

2007, APRIL, PITTSBURGH, PA: After my mother's sixth operation (another stent) my brother—who's moved back to Pittsburgh post-college, who now lives in an apartment owned by my grandfather and pays his "rent" by running errands for his Pap—accuses me, when we've returned to our parents' house, of "abandoning the family." In fact, he screams this. So I throw my suitcase across the living room. I scream back. Then I realize, forty minutes later, that I must go into that luggage to find my bottle of cortisol, which I have a hard time opening because my hands are numb and shaking.

2007, MAY, WASHINGTON, DC: Sitting on my couch a month later, I receive word, via phone, that I've won a one-year, ten-thousand-dollar salary. The salary is a fellowship from my graduate school that will allow me to stay at home and write whatever I want. For months, everyone in my insular program has taken this ten-thousand-dollar salary very seriously. We've become predictably competitive, which means that although the salary is technically low enough to qualify its recipient for government assistance—is actually less than what I'd make if I stayed on my student stipend—and I'm not permitted to work anywhere else while I have it, for reasons of pure ego I'm ecstatic about the news (*yer goddamn right*).

Within the hour I fall sick with joy. Very sick, but not in the way that I'm now accustomed to. It has the marshy, tight feel of a common cold, only staggeringly magnified. Every limb sinks. My head clogs with snot, my temperature spikes, and my face begins a steady, painful throb that worsens when I move. Even my eyes hurt. So I drive slowly to my primary care physician's office, the young woman with the fancy laptop, who arrives very late to the exam room.

"Look, hey, I am so, so sorry," she says as she enters. I'm on the exam table in a pair of track pants. I'm holding my sick head to the sky to keep blood from running to it, staring at the corrugated Plexiglas of the fluorescent lights above me. When I see my physician—typically loose and friend-like, "Hey dude," etc.—she's now timid and solemn, like someone might act after hitting your parked car.

"What are you sorry about?"

"I should have told you this earlier," she says. "I'm sorry—I said that, right? That I'm sorry?—but I was never really comfortable dealing with all these hormone medications . . ."

She goes on to say that she's been changing the dosage on the prescriptions Dr. Anatoli has been filtering through her office, "here and there." I'm too clogged with face pain to listen to which prescriptions she "tweaked," or why, or for how long.

"Ok, it's all going to be fine, I'm going to be fine," I tell her. She seems to need generosity of spirit here. "Just give me a script for some decongestant or whatever so that I can not feel like I feel right now, and I'll take care of the rest, ok?"

Immediately after, I speak to Dr. Anatoli on the phone.

On his decree, we decide that I should find a new physician, and that all prescription dosages and refills will now go solely through him.

"But Skuh-*leez*-ay," he says. "For situations like this and many others, you really must have a medical bracelet. You really must."

2008, JANUARY, NEW ORLEANS, LA: A day into my thirtieth birthday celebration weekend (what friends called a "bro-down"; what Loren called a "man-date"), I determine there is food poisoning in my bloodstream. Maybe it's from oysters, maybe not, but it triggers an ugly, purging reflex in my body and rejects every substance I attempt to ingest, including cortisol and levothyroxine. I spend the weekend not in the French Quarter, drinking hurricanes and eulogizing my twenties, but in a dark hotel room a few blocks off, watching a local access show starring an old Cajun man with an eye patch.

Dr. Anatoli, weeks later, when I return to DC: "We had a young man, a student, younger than you. Hypopituitary, like you. Went out for a night with his friends. Drinks of alcohol. Passed out to sleep in his dorm room without taking his cortisol medication and, Skuh-*leez*-ay, he did not wake up. This is why you must *go to the emergency room when this happens,* and *you must have a bracelet—*"

There were more episodes like that. Each one pressed a fresh dent in me. By thirty-one I'd turned hesitant and nervous in an undignified way I hadn't been before. This was particularly true of new experiences, where the smallest gaps in confidence opened the door just enough for gusts of untamable stress to blow through, and I grew more and more alert to, and paranoid about, which gust would be the one I couldn't withstand.

Newness, something I'd always craved, became a source of dread. After graduate school I bounced from job to job for two years, collecting gigs like I always had, teaching then writing then teaching writing, sometimes for big, well-known companies and sometimes for very small ones with big ideas, the kind that required the type of ruthless dedication and output I had in spades in New York. But now that kind of exhaustion only drove me toward an inner fracture. Even the smallest obstacles—flash arguments with people at the post office, mix-ups with work vendors—triggered the same kind of fight-or-flight paralysis as the events of my wedding had. Then anxiousness about potential episodes became stress-inducing events in themselves, driving me numb-handed and weary.

At thirty-two I took a job at an organization I'd worked hard for two years to help found, a free writing center for DC school students. I loved the people and the work, which felt noble in the way that only truly low-paying work can seem. A month into the job, after mistakenly missing a deadline—I was a day late on an insignificant update to our website—I was reprimanded firmly by my supervisor. I'd made mistakes at the children's publisher, ones that drained chunks of budget money and reset schedules, far worse oversights than a delayed website post. Yet I fell ill immediately afterward, calling out sick for days, pumping cortisol, humming with weakness about the prospect of making another error and what bodily response that might yield.

When I made mistakes at the children's publisher I'd apologize, fix things, and keep moving. But now even a tersely worded email, or the lack of a response to one, triggered an episode or gave way to shuddering illness. My body would stop. I'd cancel everything, call my boss and say—what? What could I tell her? Anyone? It was all so vague and dubious-sounding, I knew it as I was saying it—*I have this problem? With my hormones?*—wondering about the psychosomatics, knowing full well that stress was as physiological as it was physical, that I had the same capability to create it as I did to avoid it, that one fed the other.

During my high school swimming days we had one guy on the team, a middling breaststroker a few years older than me, who claimed to have Osgood-Schlatter's in his knee joints. His version of the disorder always seemed to make itself known only during the final moments of a close race: the moment he came off that last turn, four lanes of teenagers stabbing the water with prayer-clasped hands, each within a quarter-body-length of the other, Jane McCarty with a clipboard on the sidelines screaming "PULL! PULL!" Every time, my teammate would pull up in those last few yards, screaming and wincing in agony as someone from another lane, another team, jutted forth to beat him. Then the guy would slowly, dramatically climb from the pool and curl up on the deck holding his suddenly pain-stricken knee, goggles around his neck, red-faced, calling desperately for ice and the trainer.

I never liked that guy. But by thirty-two, that's exactly who I felt like.

The rules I'd made for myself in crafting a disaster story were designed, at least in part, to exert the illusion of control over my illness, which swirled below my skin in ways I could never truly harness. Owning parts of my illness, steering what people knew and how they saw me in relation to it, was all I could do to assume authority over it. I was good at that part.

But by thirty-two my only means for control over my illness's prime export—stress, the threat of it—became ruthless preparation, a constant surveying of hypotheticals and anticipations, a steady, frightened life math. I made lists. Compilations of very simple tasks that I needed to complete each day. Like the rules I'd concocted in New York, the lists shrunk things down. I had them everywhere: at work, at home, in the car, helping me see an end to work toward.

In the early days, in New York, tenacity was my control mechanism. I could perform my big, fat disaster story and feel strong as a result. I could go off of testosterone for months without a thought, almost on a whim, and convince myself that it was in the service of *becoming*, developing a language for the man I'd be.

By thirty-two I *was* that man, and the only language I seemed able to develop was the language of my limits, the set of boundaries I seemed, always, to be drawing and redrawing. Awareness of those boundaries reversed something in me. I needed to learn a different, defensive brand of control, a constant, unending attempt to dodge or block all potential signs of a brand new catastrophe.

To put it another way: I never missed being able to swim two and a half lengths underwater. I missed, dearly, the days when I didn't know that I couldn't.

At thirty-three, nine years after I should have, I got the medical emergency bracelet. There wasn't any one event that triggered it. Like Loren's and my decision to get married, logic piled up and aligned and made a fine enough case for itself, and I gave in to it with the same colicky reluctance.

OK. Fine.

My bracelet is from a website that advertises itself as "one of the foremost designers of contemporary medical emergency bracelets." My model: the "Rubber ID, Classic style," has a thin, watch-like, black rubber wristband and a long stainless steel amulet and caduceus, engraved on its underside like this:

ADRENAL INSUFFICIENCY

STEROIDS

MIKE SCALISE

I did not love the bracelet. It felt clunky and alien on my wrist. It got caught on Loren's shirt when I was in the throes of removing it. The stainless steel on the rubber wristband snagged the material on our couch. I made sure it was tucked, always, beneath my shirtsleeve, away from anyone who could see it. I'd long stopped telling people about my tumor, at least in the way I once had. Now I shared details begrudgingly and vaguely, hesitant to waste people's time with the tale.

"Weird hormone thing," was as embellished as I got.

I often think about why the story died in me, and why I mourned the telling of it. Had I changed that much in nine years? I'd always thought a catastrophe's greatest power was its ability to freeze time. I'd always wondered if we moved, marker to marker, through life like this; disaster to disaster, earning change only when we've suffered enough for it. *Drowning, tumor, no hormones,* then—waiting and disaster prep? Over-planning and evasion? *Take extra cortisol pills for your public reading so you don't go into adrenal crisis and die. Take an extra half a pill when you land in Pittsburgh for Thanksgiving, before you see your family, so you don't go into adrenal crisis and die. That event sounds stressful—get out of it. This job is overwhelming. Quit it.* In the early days I endured a disaster, then moved on to tell the tale of it. I made it mine, or at least appeared to. Now I was unmoored and tentative, divorced from that time, part of me glad and bidding it good riddance, but another, louder part of me wishing, like that sad-eyed poet, that I could return to my lovely tenure under its full influence. I'd felt stronger then, more capable. The world felt, in small ways, malleable. I didn't know it was possible to both rue something and long deeply for it in the same steady breath.

CH. 23

CRAZY LADY

The first thing my father showed Loren and me when we got to the dock were the stitches on his palm. My father, my mother, and my brother had spent the morning at an ER in Pasadena, Maryland—forty minutes from DC—not far from where my parents had chosen to dock their new yacht, a green-and-white 45-footer, the same yacht whose slipcover had ripped through the inside of my father's hand when he tried to remove it that morning. The bandage was slapped across his hand.

"Why didn't you guys call me?" I asked.

"All fixed! No need!" my father said. He was fueling the boat, maneuvering a tube, sweat-sogged and tan and incurably nervous. The dock was at the end of a gravel road in an otherwise nondescript suburb, and had around its quarters a blue maintenance hangar and a seafood restaurant with a vast wooden deck. The cove was quiet and smelled like weak shore-line and diesel. As my father finished fueling, my brother, the apparent deckhand, climbed across the boat's bow collecting lassos of rope as through he knew what he was doing with them, wearing what he later called "boat shoes," untying the rope (and the boat) from its convoluted loops around various poles, updating my mother on his progress. My mother was rooting around the hull behind the steering mechanism above us, smoking, saying something about a "dinghy."

"Are we supposed to help?" I asked Loren.

"I have no idea how that would even work," she said.

So we stood on the dock, watching the rest of my family slide around and prepare as we might watch contestants on a reality television game show.

"Did you see your father's latest battle wound?" my mother yelled down, laughing.

To this my father, bent low, unhooked the fuel line from his new sea vessel, then, to no one in particular, raised the middle finger on his freshly stitched hand.

The story of my parents and the yacht was now roughly two weeks old. My mother had broken the news to me matter-of-factly, over the phone. It occurred to me later that if I hadn't called to check in on other matters, that she might never have told me about the purchase at all.

"Well, we bought a boat," she said.

For at least ten minutes we'd been talking (about her tomato trellises, about my brother), and it was almost as if she'd forgotten about the boat, as if the act of fulfilling a years-long dream had demoted it to an afterthought.

"*Holy shit*," I said.

"We're going to get it this weekend," she said.

"This," I said, "is exciting?"

"Yeah," she told me, an off-balance flatness to her voice, "I guess it is."

The logistics behind the purchase of the boat, I learned over the next few minutes, were as follows: In recent months, and with surprisingly little dissent, the co-working faction of my family had agreed to sell our nearly sixty-year-old heating and air-conditioning firm to a larger, more expansive corporate entity with a meaningless neo-biz name like RiteVac. The corporation would maintain the firm, its name, and many of its employees as a new part of their growing cache of "mechanical and electrical construction, energy infrastructure, LEED construction, design/build, life safety, and facilities services."

I'd heard vague conversational echoes about the buyout during Christmas the previous year. It wasn't something anyone seemed particularly aggravated or saddened by. My grandfather was in his eighties now, far from his days as an influential voice in the daily goings-on. His attention had turned sharply to my grandmother who, after a bout of congestive heart failure two years earlier, had swiftly and sadly declined, both mentally and physically, lost to dementia's endless corridor. She now rarely ate, threw her food across the room like an infant. She had afternoon-long spells of deep paranoia, suspended in the mental state of some earlier version of herself: screaming, hitting my grandfather, convinced that someone had stolen her newborn (my father). My father would have to talk with her, convince her over a phone line that no, he was not stolen, but had rather become an adult human, which only served to frighten my grandmother more.

The scattered, heartsick opinions about what should be done about my grandmother and her health wore the same kind of wedge into my father's side of the family as they had for my mother and her siblings after their own mother's stroke so many years before. For her part, my mother remained contentedly silent on the matter, spending days helping my grandmother where she could. But mostly my mother watched, almost morbidly amused, as the same type of theater played itself out with the same dissolute results. Some lobbied for a convalescent home, some for second opinions as to her state. Siblings stopped speaking to each other. And my grandfather, as he always had, refused all suggestions and went instead with gut economics, bringing in in-home, cut-rate nursing candidates to work with my grandmother, only to fire them weeks later when they were too inept, or too overweight, or, most often, for blackness he couldn't force himself to accept. ("Tell me," he'd said during an impromptu phone call in the fall of 2009, seemingly day-drunk, "how am I supposed to feel about this *Obama*.")

Amidst this clamoring sense of familial decline, my uncle, the reigning president of the heating and AC firm, saw the opportunity for certain shifts prudent for long-term survival. At Christmas, while my now bone-frail grandmother screamed in blank terror at the strangers in her home, my uncles, father, and grandfather sat at the kitchen table speaking in acronyms and projections, evaluating possible buyers of their collective life's work.

Before the sale was finalized, the new corporate officials dispatched management auditors to evaluate the workflow, the value and promise of current executives, which is to say that the auditors were gauging the worth of my father and his brothers.

What the corporate auditors found, my mother told me, was that my father was deemed an alarmingly valuable asset to the organization.

"Holy shit," I said.

He received a settlement to entice him to stay with the company and share his knowledge, my mother told me. The sum was enough, she said, to buy a yacht and the fuel for it and a dock space to put it in.

"Holy shit," I said. "Holy shit, holy shit, holy shit."

My mother and I had spoken some weeks before, quite seriously and soberly, about recent news regarding yet another stent, this one through a different, over-blocked artery in her neck, more threatening than the one before. It was all of the same phrases and buzzwords we'd heard for over a decade now, each time my mother submitted to another scraping-through of her pulmonary wiring. This time, though, she wasn't quite sold.

"I'm going to another doctor," she'd said. "This is bullshit."

She'd sounded tired. She was nearing sixty now, and the prospect of subjecting her well-worn body to more procedures didn't seem to provoke the kind of dread for her that it once had. Now it was just exasperation, an unsettling, soft kind of surrender. We'd left the conversation at the same place we'd started it: her with the looming threat of a repeat performance, me wondering for how long this could happen, when, after so long, her last performance might be.

But now: the boat (the boat!), which had, it seemed, replaced or waylaid the looming concern about her neck artery that was or was not dangerously clogged. My parents had bought the boat without telling the rest of my father's side of the family. My mother made it a point to tell me this; she'd said, "We're not telling them." They'd purchased it, used, at a marina in North Carolina, and were flying down that weekend to pick it up. Jim and Joan, their retired, childless dream-models, had agreed to meet them there, at the point of purchase, then accompany my parents on the week-plus trip north on an intracoastal waterway that cut through and up the Eastern shoreline, to patiently educate their old high school buddies in the rigors of steering, the nuances of a dual motor, how to navigate waterways, how to drop anchor, and how, finally, to dock for good just outside of Washington, DC.

According to my mother, over the course of that two weeks my father had:

Fallen into the intracoastal waterway, twice

Lost use of his cell phone as a result

Hyperextended his hip while docking

Abandoned, abruptly and at high speed, the boat's steering

mechanism as it approached a tight corridor in the intra-coastal waterway, causing Jim and Joan to rush in, frantically, to take over, at which point my father banished himself to the back of the boat's hull, where he sat for hours smoking, apologizing.

And now, hand-stitches from the slipcover, which prevented my father from steering the boat from the fueling station to my parents' designated slip, some four hundred yards of slow, careful maneuvering. So the task went to my mother. She said she'd steered the yacht a few times on the ride up from North Carolina, but always with Jim and Joan close by, and she had never once docked the thing, had only watched concerned as my father struggled, tore wide the joint of his hip, plunged fully clothed into mud-clouded waters.

"And *I*, don't *know*, what I'm *do*-ing," she said in a low, pet-rified sing-song as we all loaded into the boat: my brother and Loren sitting with me directly behind her, my nervous, beaten father toward the back, still quiet, lighting another cigarette. Docking a boat that size required little throttle beyond the slow spurt from the idling engines, a seesaw of power and stoppage from both the right and left sides, and my mother was, despite her nerves, smooth, careful and adept at the whole thing, which seemed, when I envisioned myself doing it, frightening to the core.

She was impressive to watch, but I shouldn't have been sur-prised. My mother was the most skilled, resourceful driver I'd ever known, regardless of the vehicle. My father—a lifelong Formula One fan—had, throughout the years, backed into telephone poles, drifted into snow banks and highway medians, collided four-doors into busy intersections. But my mother remained accident-less. As she docked the boat (slowly, perfectly) my brother, Loren and I stood, then delivered the woman a well-paced standing O.

"*Nice fucking work*, Mom," I said, and my brother said something similar, Loren after that. The only person who didn't say anything was my father, who remained at the back of the boat, forearms across his sooted kneecaps, head down, silent, shaken in a way that seemed unwise to approach. My mother looked happy but overwhelmed, shaking her head, breathing hard and laughing, like she'd just stepped out of the path of a blistering freighter.

"Just about had a nervous breakdown!" she said.

My brother told her she "fucking killed it," and I agreed.

"Can't feel my hands," she said, and I watched her shake them the same way I shook my own, pumping her fingers into fists.

An hour later, when a red-bearded decal pro came by to affix to the old boat its new name—my mother dubbed it THE CRAZY LADY, because, as she put it, "I have to be a crazy lady to buy this goddamn thing"—she was reminiscing about the docking of the boat as though it had happened years back: a distant, great victory that she previously couldn't envision, still making fists: in and out, in and out.

"*Still* numb in my hands," my mother said, several times, almost to herself. "Still can't feel 'em."

I knew what was happening in her body, which hormones were responding to what. I told her to make it small, to breathe slowly, and to concentrate on one breath to the next, each breath a new one, as if that tactic had ever—even once—worked for me.

I had, through all of this, been considering a foot operation. After a near decade of fitting my wide, fat acromegalic feet in sneakers and loafers, I now had side-bent big toes on both feet, painful bunions that swelled in the swampy, DC summer air to the point where I limped, sometimes doubled-over, a surge of pain through my foot like a skewer. I wanted to explore corrective surgery—when I told my father this, he said, "I have a vice, a hammer, and a chisel in the garage. Come on over whenever"—which meant for the first time leaning on my well-chosen, entirely useless primary care physician on Capitol Hill for a referral that wasn't, for once, endocrine-related.

But it also was. As with any procedure now (or even trips to the dentist, for that matter), Dr. Anatoli and his endocrine team had to be consulted regarding my hormonal management before, after, and, most importantly, during any planned work on my body. To have a bunion removed—the angle of my toes so sharp and mangled that the bent bones of my foot would likely have to be shattered and reset—would trigger a torrent of stress that my bloodstream couldn't bear on its own.

But in addition to the hormonal prep, my useless physician wanted blood tests, the first I'd had in nine years that gauged something other than GHRH levels and testosterone. The tests were basic. A "matter of protocol," my doctor said, designed to check my cholesterol levels as I moved into my thirties.

I wasn't worried. For the first time since nearly drowning in high school, I was swimming again on the regular. Like everything else now it was regimented, planned to dodge any and all forms of mental and physical stress. 1500 yards. Three times a week. A high-to-moderate "aerobic" pace. One minute break every 500 yards. Breaths every four strokes. 100 yards cool down. No exceptions.

And sadly, achingly, sex had become like this too, though certainly not by design. The feverish bouts of the previous decade had cooled now in ways I hadn't noticed, even on T— five pumps daily now of AndroGel, on my arm and belly both. Throughout the near decade, and despite all my lingering paranoia, there'd been little to no break in Loren's brand of support. As I changed, she changed, or, as needed, refused to. She either complimented whatever new predicament my illness slid forth, or found a way to provide a much-needed backbone for it. The few issues we did clash on—the hospital pajamas, going to Mark McKiernan's wedding, which to this day Loren calls the actions of a "complete fucking dipshit"—produced little more than a snide remark, an earnest request. But now, after many weeks of unintended sexlessness—and a thorny, sullen distance that grew between us as a result—Loren approached me teary and frustrated on a Saturday to ask, plainly: Why didn't I *want* her anymore?

I *did*, as much as always, more than always. But the idea of *want*, for my body, had become a strangely itinerant thing. In a bloodstream full of healthy male hormones, testosterone (and with it, libido) begins to wane post-thirty. The body's receptors for lust begin their slow retirement. I had been, to varying degrees, holding off that retirement for a decade. But now it slipped away from me in ways I could no longer be trusted to notice. So when it came for sex with my wife—someone who had, through the last decade, found ways to grow more inviting with her angles, aging with grace and beauty, sure, but also with an allure and power that made her sharper, more confident—there were certainly still moments where I felt pulled hard into her, where our lips met and the mere press of her made my skin itch for hers. And the sex, when we had it, was far more satisfying than it had been ten years before, when my hormones had been at full throttle. Our frequencies, in that sense, were carefully tuned to each other in a way they'd never been. But my body seemed less willing or capable to *find* that frequency as often as it once had. It was the first time Loren and I had been truly encroached upon by my lack of T in a way I hadn't engineered, and counteracting it required concentration. Maintenance. I needed to put sex on a regimen. So we did. After work. On weekends. In the mornings, when my hormones were newly ingested, at full strength. I started keeping a mental tally, heartbroken and embarrassed that love, as it aged, required it.

There had been more repairs, more preparations, more measures of complete safety. I'd quit smoking for longer than I ever had before, and aside from the spotty libido, in many ways I began again to feel like the me who'd been buried by time and circumstance. I was still pale and misshapen, galoompy and round-gutted, Roman nose and patches of gray hair. But I'd lost significant weight for the first time in ten years. Some of the GH-influenced angles of my head seemed to soften and recede. In tiny ways, I got a version of my looks back, or better, I looked like someone I hadn't looked like before. For nearly a year it had been like this. *Boring* was, in its unexciting way, almost working.

The results of the cholesterol test: astronomical.

"You said that your father has had heart problems?" my useless doctor asked.

"My *mother*," I said. "We've talked about this."

And we had, just days before, in depth, about my mother's heart history, about her sister, about her father. I had watched him write it down.

"What does your father have then?" he asked.

"I never mentioned my father."

"No, I think you did . . ."

And so on.

Within minutes I was squatted on a curb in Capitol Hill, my mother's voice in my cell phone. I hadn't wanted to tell her. From the moment I heard my triglyceride count I wanted, through some lingering sense of illness pride, to keep this information from my mother at all costs. Unlike with a tumor that bursts on your brain, heart problems—or the threat of them—are so capable of placing the people who have them under the hard light of personal neglect: it's *your* living choices that led to the problems, *your* responsibility to change in order to extinguish them. I'd seen this, fallen victim to it. And with my mother's impressive wealth of experience in matters cardiopulmonary—she of the near-yearly procedure, of the barely held-to diet, of itinerant exercise—I envisioned a lecture ("I *told* you to not be like me"), or a rickety tutor-pupil dynamic that I simply couldn't accept. I was still convinced, after all these years, even after my many failures to care for my own health's future, that in our chess game of dueling illnesses, *I* was the better sick person. But my physician wanted to know which medications my mother had taken, if she'd had adverse effects from any of them, information which would allow him to assign me yet another pill and supplement to add to my daily intake, which would now look like this:

Five pumps, AndroGel (10 g)
One pill, levothyroxine (125 mcg)
Two .5 pills, cortisol (10 mg)
One pill, Simvastatin (20 mg)
One capsule, fish and/or flaxseed oil (1000 mg)
One tablet, male-oriented multivitamin (measurement indeterminable)

"Ah, *dammit*," my mother said when I told her, as though she'd just dropped her keys through the bars of a sewer grate. "You know that none of this is your fault, right?"

I wasn't sure, then, that I agreed. I was angry, far angrier than I'd been in response to my tumor diagnosis. I felt enlisted, trapped. My mother talked about her diet, about how she'd been well below critical, cholesterol-wise, for going on four years. She told me good books to buy, what foods to avoid.

"Loren's a vegetarian, Mom. We eat very well."

She talked about exercise.

"Mom. I swim."

It went on like this, her being generous, me snapping back. I may just as well have just told my mother, each time, like a scorned teen: *I am not you.* But the evidence had proved otherwise. No matter. My mother let it all pass by her, unchallenged. She gave it room, waited for me to cool.

"We got it in the blood, Mikey," she said. "We trail it around with us."

It sounded low and kind and sorry when she said it, like something a friend might say.

"It's not so bad," she said. "You just have to take pills. You know how to do that."

"My body," I told her, "is a repository for them."

She laughed.

"Well *hell*," she said, sounding southern, like her own mother once had. "I guess that makes us both repositories."

"To human repositories," I said.

"To human repositories," she said back.

CH. 24

PRACTICE

My mother's phone number appeared first on my cell, then on Loren's. It was Friday, mid-September of 2011, weeks after our last discussion. Loren and I were couch-bound, midway through an unimpressive movie that we'd ordered through a cable box. The time was just after 10:00 P.M., well past when I refused to pick up my mother's calls—I knew she and my father were arriving at the boat that weekend, that it was only my parents, the Chesapeake, and a locker of cheap booze—so I asked Loren to ignore the second call like I had the first, expecting it to be some regressive form of my mother's voice, slow and wallowed and unchangeable.

"It's your dad," Loren said when she checked the voicemail. "He sounds strange. Call him."

Seconds later he was breathless and weak on the line.

It sounded like he was running.

"Your mother," my father said, then took a deep, fast gasp, "your mother's fallen . . . um—*fuck. Fuck.* She fell into the boat engine."

I stood in my living room.

My father was wheezing.

I think I said, *What?*

"Paramedics are going to take her to Maryland University— wait, no, *shit*—shock and trauma, I think," my father said. Then he called over, I imagined, to a nearby paramedic and asked: "Where are we going again?"

"Dad—"

"—University of Maryland Shock and Trauma Center," he said, and I heard sirens cry over the line, a rustling of things, a slamming of others. "Baltimore. I'm following the ambulance in the car—"

"DAD," I said. "WHAT HAPPENED."

My mother is dead, I thought. And the thought emerged to me calmly, stayed with me as a refrain as I told Loren to grab two pillows, as I went to the daily divider that contained my many pills, both new and old, and put it in a backpack, as I took an extra half a pill of cortisol, stashed some for later. *My mother is dead.* We put the pillows in the car. We drove on the Baltimore-Washington Parkway at ninety-one miles an hour. I spoke to my brother. I said, "Something's happened to Mom on the boat, I don't know what, but *do not leave Pittsburgh until I get there and find out the problem.*"

"Don't leave me out," my brother said. "You guys always leave me out."

My mother is dead. I braced for the moment and its electric heft to drape a blanket over me, for my blood to poison itself with its absences. But that didn't happen. I was calm and resolute and advancing, like I'd been as a teen lifeguard, detached, moving fast toward distress, reflexively, weaving around sedans and pickups, phoning friends in Baltimore, lining up a foldout couch for Loren and me to sleep on that night, because our stay in the hospital, I knew, would be brief.

I thought often in the months after about why this moment and my hormones didn't decimate me like so many other, smaller moments had. Why this, of all moments, was so manageable, why could I cut through it so quickly, with no list, no preparation, everything new and horrible failing to cause its usual, wicked stir. *My mother is dead* were the only words I could think, and there was no hysteria woven through them, no menace to their power.

It occurred to me only recently that I had, in fact, been rigorously prepared for what had happened that night. We all had. We'd been practicing this moment for over a decade.

My mother was not dead. My brother followed up with a calmer, more lucid version of my father, then reported back to Loren and me as we moved on the parkway, slowed down to a safer pace, exhaled.

Here is what my brother reported: my mother and father had arrived at the marina in Pasadena, Maryland, at just after

9:00 P.M. My mother, with no flashlight, stepped into the boat's cabin, after which my father heard screams. The maintenance worker who had been repairing the boat's engine had left the doors to it open, like two split halves of a ribcage, which meant that where a floor should have been, there was a multi-foot sink into a web of nautical machinery. My mother fell hard into it, slapped into the engine well face-first, shattering her femur, breaking two ribs, and partially flattening a lung.

In the University of Maryland Shock and Trauma Unit in Baltimore, my mother had a weight suspended, a lever, ringlike, hanging at the bottom of her ER gurney, stabilizing her newly cracked leg. I saw it, imagined the weight dropping to the floor, snapping her small frame like a carrot. She was unconscious by the time we got there, held together with bandages and tubes, her ER doctors holding off on all major re-shifting procedures, waiting to impale her joints with a bridgework of metal rods until they talked to her cardiologists, determined what they could and couldn't do in order to repair her.

Now past midnight, there was enough of a stall that Loren could put her head down on a pillow in the outpatient visitor's lounge, and my father and I could step onto the barren Baltimore street outside the Shock and Trauma Center for a solemn, impatient cigarette.

It was, in these instances, what we did.

"I'm scheduled for an MRI next week," my father told me.

"Wait, *you* are?" I asked.

My father told me he'd been having cognitive diversions, forgetting things, seeing luminescent images, shimmering slats in his vision field at random daytime hours. He felt unbalanced and almost weightless during these times, he told me, thrown into a kind of mind-limp tumble, convinced it was a neurological hiccup.

In the two-plus months since they'd docked the Crazy Lady in Maryland, my father refused to steer the vessel. When they did take the boat out, my mother was the captain, and gladly so. Her spirits, in those weeks, had climbed to a pitch of joy higher than I'd ever seen from her. She planned excursions. She wore a captain's hat. It was moving and confounding. I talked to Loren about this for hours after each dock visit—"What do you think it is?"—curious and proud yet gravely concerned. She simply didn't discuss (or even appear to think about) her heart issues any longer, which, to my knowledge, remained perfectly unresolved, that artery in her neck maybe/possibly/probably damming up slowly, more dangerously by the day. No matter. There was zero news of that now, and the absence of this kind of rhetoric when we talked left me stunned, unsure of what to say. It was the boat and only the boat now. On it, my mother had bloomed into someone who was wide-smiled and confident, with a pride and lightness I hadn't witnessed since I was very young.

But my father, for his part, had lost all footing in that regard. He still hadn't told his family about the purchase (that, I imagined now, was about to change). When I'd call, midweek, regarding their weekend plans, my father would halt talks of their boating itinerary to tell me that when he thought about the boat, and tending to it, his hands began to tremble, that there was a drop in his gut that tightened and turned as they got closer to the dock. When Loren and I came to visit them my father was increasingly distant, ruined with unease, far worse than he'd been the day he tore his palm open.

"I'm snake-bit by this boat," he'd say.

And now the boat, this whole experiment, had broken my mother as well.

"I'm thinking about this boat, and I don't know, Mike," he said while we were on that street in Baltimore.

He blew smoke from his nostrils, raised his eyes, for a beat only, to the star-blank night. Sedans rolled slow on the road next to us. I wondered if he was thinking what I was, even as I was ashamed to be thinking it. I wondered if he was considering, as I now did, that perhaps he and my mother's true apex of aptitude was merely to have dreams, but not to live them.

"Things need to change," my father said.

I nodded sympathetically, sucked in at the filter. I wanted to say that there was no shame in retiring this narrative, that he could fold it up like a map and head in another direction and that would be okay. I wanted to hug my father. I thought about putting my arms out. But in these instances this was not what we did, so I held them dumbly at my sides as I exhaled, watched the smoke from my throat flap and split like dryer exhaust against the bulb of a dim, orange streetlamp.

"I think, after all this," he said to me, "we might need to get a different boat."

CH. 25

A UNIVERSE OF NO ACCIDENTS

ho were the rules for? They were for anyone who had
something horrible and tangled weave through
their life, looking for a teeny bit of control over it.
Jesus, I thought for years. Who wouldn't want *that*?

It was, I know now—I've known for some time—supreme bullshit. It was posturing, a cover-up. I wrote and lived those rules for one person: my mother, my rival in personal catastrophe. I wanted to show her a way to be sick other than the way she'd relied on, which drove her so sullen and stomped-on, drove us so mad with helplessness. What I did was meant to be a template, *her* template, to take from me in hopes that she could cull some sense of joy from her disaster, that she could revel—not in dying of her lineage, obviously, but in finding her own, ingenious way to keep living through it, to take a boastful, basking pride in remaining defiantly, obnoxiously, not-dead.

Because under that thin illusion of victory: I had fun. It's such amazing fun to feel right, even if you're not, to allow to yourself to become hypnotized by your own defense mechanisms, to create a character for yourself. When I got to pierce the stale air of a conversation with the words "Dr. Sunshine" I felt like I'd slapped a leash across the neck of every fucked detail that happened to me, then tugged hard, put it in its place. And it becomes possible, in that complicated role-play, to grow infatuated with something, even as it destroys you.

That illusion doesn't fade easily, either. I still say it, any time I find myself caught in a conversation with someone where I allow the details of my illness to get past vague basics, when their head cocks to the side and the questions come.

"Those first years," I tell them, "I kind of really loved it."

During her stay at the University of Maryland Shock and Trauma Unit, it became clear that my mother didn't need my help. At least not anymore. On day two, the first day she was truly conscious—she'd been fogged over by morphine and other pain-blurring medications—I took the train up from DC to find her sitting upright in her bed in the ICU, nested by snoozing monitors and metal boxes, an oxygen mask upon her face to aide the shallow, painful breaths that her broken ribs and flattened lung had restricted her to.

"*Darth*," she said through the mask, in a billowy voice, "*I am your father.*"

I could see her smiling through the mask.

"You mean *Luke*?" I asked.

"*No*," she said, still deep voiced.

Then:

"*Oh. Wait. Shit. Sorry. LUKE, I am your father . . .*"

My mother gave shit to the entire nursing staff. They were young, impeccably skilled and patient, and she roasted each like an insult comic.

"Did you come in here to screw up my IV again?" she'd say, or: "Oh, I like this one. Everyone, look. It's Captain Bedpan!" Estimates from her surgeons were that my mother wouldn't be able to walk on her own for at least six months, four months if her bones and muscle growth responded well to intense, twice-weekly physical therapy sessions, which my brother, from his reluctant post in Pittsburgh, had already set up at a facility near their house for when she returned.

"They're putting me on a walker," she'd say. "But after that I get a cane, which is good, because then I can beat your father across the head with it."

I found I looked forward to visits, to sitting with her in her room, quiet, watching my mother conduct her stay in the ICU. She was by now a pro, in her element, and I had no reference point for how to respond. Neither did my father. Yet he began to loosen as the days passed—or, my mother's pleasantness began to loosen him, good-humored and silly as she was removed from oxygen, as her lung regained full function, as the rods were pulled from her leg—and he seemed to enjoy himself almost as much as my mother appeared to. We watched football games together, cheering snidely for the Steelers among the other patients and visitors, so many of them wearing, like uniforms, some form of Raven purple. Jim and Joan even came out for one night to sit around my mother's bed like it was a campfire, telling disaster stories.

But when they weren't there, my mother talked about my own disaster, which was now nine years old. She seemed to psychically bind the two, and grew attuned to their differences and similarities:

"At least they put me in a single, thank god," she said. "Remember that man they put you with? Who kept taking his robe off? And his kids with the ice cream sandwiches?"

It was as though we were talking about a family vacation.

"Who was that woman who gave you the pens?" she'd ask hours later.

"Who, Jean?" I asked. "I loved Jean. Jean was awesome."

"No, no, not her. The one with the funny name."

"Oh. *Avis.*"

And so on.

She'd talk like this, about bedside care, about the tone and manner of her doctors. "Was it like this for you?" she'd ask, as if, in the nine years between then and now there had been no other hospital visits, no opportunities for my mother to consider these things, to make these pairings. As if she wasn't the weathered veteran in this racket. It confounded me, then and for months after. I couldn't get my head around it. Why *this* disaster? What was it about this fat failure that turned her so wry and easy, channeling something that resembled, in its best moments, a kind of freedom?

I tried to ask my mother this a year later, at the end of July, just after my tumor's ten-year anniversary. She was now walking at full gait, had bounced back robustly after only four months. She, my father, and I were eating soft-shell crab sandwiches on the deck of a seafood joint at a marina in Mears Point, Maryland, where they'd recently relocated the Crazy Lady. Night had just broken, and the air was warm but not thick.

"This is such a nice night," my mother said, looking over the water, a full glass of Pinot tipping into her lips. "It's just really . . . nice."

I agreed, drank nothing.

"Mom," I said, "I've been thinking. Why do you think you had such a good time in the hospital last year?"

"Oh, I don't know about a *good time*. I was on so much morphine," she said. "I couldn't breathe, I couldn't move. I was loopy. Whacked out of my brain."

"You weren't loopy the *whole* time," I said. "Toward the end you seemed to like it there."

"It did seem that way, hon," my father said.

But my mother didn't (or couldn't?) answer the question, and instead began to reminisce about her stay there, then brag about her quick-healing skills, which she'd earned. She'd earned it all. Was there any other way of seeing my mother, after all these years, as something other than Job-like? Our morbid predictions for her had all been brilliant failures. How could I see the woman, by now, as anything less than indestructible?

The night air around us was barely dented by a chill, and within seconds my question to my mother was lost to that air. I don't know if she lost interest in the question, or had moved on from it. Maybe she could do that now. Maybe my mother hadn't, like me, circled the circumstances of her boat fall for months, curious about why this disaster struck her so differently than the many, many others. Maybe she didn't spend hours trying to turn it into a parable about how this mess wasn't inherited, or knotted up in other, more complicated family entanglements. We'd both tried, in that last way at least, to make a hard push in our lives from new, different angles. Perhaps she never considered how that newness might have exposed a bittersweet vulnerability in us: a window, a portal through which catastrophe could sneak its crooked fingers in and complicate our plans, press us down, test our devotion to them.

Maybe she was free of that kind of thinking. Maybe, for my mother—casting smoke from her Marlboro out across the deck tables, still no mention of any lingering heart issues (*clogged artery, fuck it*), saying to my father and me, "This is such a nice night"—it was, finally, just an accident.

For me, there can only be a universe of no accidents. That is the only rule now, and I impose it as best I can, until the inevitable day when I won't be able to. I build the best bunker I can. My cholesterol is low. I leave at 5:00 P.M. I breathe every four strokes. My hormones enter my body in the morning, then again sometimes at night. There are rare times when they don't, but those times aren't by my design. They're the result of administrative lulls and oversights—refill request pile-ups at my specialist's office—where the pharmaceutical repository of my body goes starkly empty, which means the world does too, at least briefly. But when the world comes back, believe me: the air around me feels so full, and the people who move through it so alive, their cadences clacking at me in such a strong, clear pitch, as if someone has yanked sealed plugs from my long-jammed ears, and my wife's face is so warm, her touch such a live, deep current, and I itch so badly during those moments to tap the shoulder of someone, a stranger maybe, and say, *Jesus, just look at all this.*

But I don't. Instead I wear my bracelet, which I've become as tightly bonded to as my wedding ring. I love how it feels on my wrist, a half-advertised secret. Most times, no one notices I'm wearing it. But there is that rare occasion—in a work meeting, at a party, or at a coffee shop—where someone will mistake it for a watch, ask me for the time. And when I say I don't know—which I do, always—they'll ask me again, or, as though I'm lying, grab for the wrist I wear my bracelet on, pull it to their face. And when they see clearly that bracelet and what it might mean, their expression becomes something I recognize so well, and I get a flutter in my belly and a sly, welcome grin in my soul because I know that I can do whatever I choose to with that moment. I can tell that person anything I want.

ACKNOWLEDGMENTS

The first round of ceaseless gratitude goes to the organizations who encouraged and enabled the completion of this book: 826DC, the Bread Loaf Writers' Conference, Philip Roth and the Stadler Center for Poetry at Bucknell University, The Corporation of Yaddo, and Ross White and Matthew Olzmann, who run a simple, essential project called The Grind that aided immensely throughout the writing of this book. Massive thanks also to the Center for Fiction, Audible.com, and the rest of the selection committee for the Christopher Doheny Award. Thanks also to the resourceful, hilarious May Rose Chen for her research support, and to Dr. David Fel for the good counsel.

Round two of gratitude starts off with Janet Silver at Zachary Shuster Harmsworth, who believed in me and in this book when she had little reason to do either thing. And to Kristen Radtke, Sarah Gorham, and the crew at Sarabande Books—my god, just thank you. I did not know this kind of care and attention was possible. To my editor, Ariel Lewiton, I remain so astounded by your clear, confident vision for this book and what it could be. It's been such a pleasure syncing up on this thing.

Portions of this book have appeared in much different forms in the following publications: *Agni*, *Ninth Letter*, *Post Road Magazine*, and *The New York Times*.

Thanks for my teachers and mentors: Kyoko Mori, Geeta Kothari, Matt Klam, and Jane Brox, all of whom, in their own ways, utterly tattooed me. I'm grateful also for the advice, patience, and friendship of Dom Anselmo and Gretchen Wolfe-Anselmo, Brock Graham, Leigh Allen, Akil Kamau, Patricia Chui, Ed Molina, Daynah Burnett, Ryan Call, Joe Hall, Cheryl Quimba, Kevin Stoy, Rion Scott, Gerald Maa, Christian Anton Gerard, Justin St. Germain, Jennine Capó Crucet, Jen Percy, Joanna Pearson, Matthew Buckley Smith, Urban Waite, Will Schutt, Tania Biancalani, Porochista Khakpour, Laura van den Berg, Paul Yoon, Ted Thompson, Nina McConigley, Josh Rivkin, Cara Blue Adams, Cam Terwilliger, Kaitlyn Greenidge, Alexandria Marzano-Lesnevich, Chris Arnold, Reese Kwon, Ben Brown, Kira Wisniewski, Joe and Nell Callahan, Oliver Munday, Allyson Rudolph, Dave Madden, Lila Cecil, and Alexi Zentner.

Whew.

Big, monster love goes forever to my father, my brother, and especially my mother for teaching me how to stand up and step forward.

And finally, to Loren, my best friend and greatest love: thank you for rubbing elbows with me.

D. Leigh Allen

MIKE SCALISE'S work has appeared in *Agni, Indiewire, Ninth Letter, The New York Times, Wall Street Journal,* and other places. He's an 826DC advisory board member, has received fellowships and scholarships from Bread Loaf, Yaddo, the Ucross Foundation, and was the Philip Roth Writer in Residence at Bucknell University.

SARABANDE BOOKS is a nonprofit literary press located in Louisville, KY, and Brooklyn, NY. Founded in 1994 to champion poetry, short fiction, and essay, we are committed to creating lasting editions that honor exceptional writing. For more information, please visit sarabandebooks.org.